Nr. 7833.
40 Gramm

Nr. 7834.
65 Gramm.

Nr. 7835. 125 Gramm.

Nr. 7836. 95 Gramm.

Nr. 7856.0

The Comprehensive Guide to
Chocolate Molds
Objects of Art & Artists' Tools

Wendy Mullen

Dedication

This book is dedicated to the memory of Lorry Hanes. For many of the collectors who knew her, she was the inspiration that started them on a lifetime's journey collecting chocolate molds. Lorry will not be forgotten.

Who will speak in my absence?
Who will stand in my place?
Will you rejoice in the life that I've led?
Who will I inspire along the way?

Who will sing at my passing?
Who will dance upon my grave?
For whom will I be a lasting memory?
For whom will I easily fade?

Do I give enough?

Do I love enough?
Do I live enough?
Did I ever give up on anyone I shouldn't have?

Do I risk enough?
Do I forgive enough?
Do I trust enough?
Am I good enough?

Who will wake from this slumber?
Who will share in the faith?
That we are the sum of the choices we make?
We cannot lay down at the mercy of fate?

"Who" by Roman Morykit and Cilette Swann of Gypsy Soul
CD title "The Journey," available at GypsySoul.com
Off the Beaten Track Recordings, 2002

Library of Congress Cataloging-in-Publication Data

Mullen, Wendy.
  The comprehensive guide to chocolate molds : objects of art & artists' tools / Wendy Mullen.
      p. cm.
  Includes bibliographical references.
  ISBN 0-7643-2278-8 (hardcover)
  1. Chocolate molds—Collectors and collecting—Catalogs.
I. Title.

NK8490.M854 2005
664'.153'0284—dc22
                                          2005010493

Designed by Mark David Bowyer
Type set in Bodoni Bd BT/Souvenir Lt BT

ISBN: 0-7643-2278-8
Printed in China
1 2 3 4

Published by Schiffer Publishing Ltd.
4880 Lower Valley Road
Atglen, PA 19310
Phone: (610) 593-1777; Fax: (610) 593-2002
E-mail: Info@schifferbooks.com

For the largest selection of fine reference books on this and related subjects, please visit our web site at
www.schifferbooks.com
We are always looking for people to write books on new and related subjects. If you have an idea for a book please contact us at the above address.

This book may be purchased from the publisher.
Include $3.95 for shipping.
Please try your bookstore first.
You may write for a free catalog.

In Europe, Schiffer books are distributed by
Bushwood Books
6 Marksbury Ave.
Kew Gardens
Surrey TW9 4JF England
Phone: 44 (0) 20 8392-8585; Fax: 44 (0) 20 8392-9876
E-mail: info@bushwoodbooks.co.uk
Free postage in the U.K., Europe; air mail at cost.

Contents

Acknowledgments

I would like to extend a multitude of thanks to everyone involved with this book!

Thank you to my wonderful husband Patrick—the talented photographer. You were unbelievably patient and put up with so many "re-takes"! Thank you to my children, who were very patient and understanding about having chocolate molds all over the house. Thanks to my sisters, Debbie Trujillo and Brenda Porter, and my friends Diana Cassel and Pat Vroman, who were always encouraging me. Carolyn Byrnes—what can I say—you never give up and you are always willing to help. I will treasure our crazy adventures always!

Thank you to Monica Tinhofer for the warmth and consideration you extended to me, and for providing firsthand information regarding the Anton Reiche family history. I value the time and emotion you invested while sharing your precious memories!

Thank you to the amazing Micelli family for your incredible enthusiasm and for trusting me with your story!

All of the chocolatiers, artists, and collectors were extremely generous and wonderful. It has been my privilege to get to know and work with the following people:

Adrienne Trouw, formerly of Holland Handicrafts
Anne Launius of HollyRidgeStudio.com
Audrey Reiche-Ruggieri
Betsy Schoettlin of SerendipityChocolates.com
Bill Stallings of Confectionery Antiques in Portland
Bruce and Lorry Hanes of DadsFollies.com
Carolyn Byrnes of OldMolds.com
Carolyn Deschenes of ChalkwareCollectibles.com
Cilette Swann and Roman Morykit of GypsySoul.com
Debbee Thibault of Debbeethibault.com
Diane Cazalet of ConfectioneryAntiques.com
Diane Cheffy of Santa-Sampler.com
Elle Dean
Erwin and Monika Gschwind
Faith Timberlake of TimberlakeCandies.com
Gary and Judi Vaillancourt of Valfa.com
Ginny Betourne of TroutCreekFolkArt.com
Jamie Badore of FantazticCreations.com
Jason Kaderli of EmkayMachinery.com
Kathryn Campbell of BittersweetHouse.com
Kathi Bejma Walnut Ridge Classics, also KDVintage.com
Laure Dorchy author of *The Chocolate Mould*
Lynea Lefler-Harrison of CalicoChocolates.com
Madame Irène Dorchy
Micelli Chocolate Mold Company of Micelli.com
Moni Marceau of MonisFolkArt.com
Monica Tinhofer; information for the Chocolate Mold Museum at Rammenau Castle can be found at Barockschloss-rammenau.com. If you would like to lend molds to the museum, please call: 004314869083 (Austria).
Paul and Fredricka Schwanka
Penny Burns of PennysChalkware.com
Rex Morgen of MorgenChocolate.com
Rita Reiche-Schwartz, AntonReiche@bellsouth.net
Robert J. Twardzik of RJTConfections.com
Susan Brack of TheEnchantedSleigh.com
Wendy Stys-Van Eimeren of Pineberrylane.com
William Timberlake M.D. (Dorothy Timberlake Mold Museum, New Hampshire; 13,000 chocolate, candy, and ice cream molds. By appointment only, 603-447-2671)

I love to talk about antique chocolate molds and look forward to meeting new chocolate mold enthusiasts. Please contact me through my website: www.VictorianChocolateMolds.com

—Wendy Mullen

Introduction
Chocolate Molds —
Incredible Objects of Art

Not only are the delightfully detailed pieces of chocolate that emerge from chocolate molds considered art, the molds created to achieve these miracles in chocolate are also breathtaking works of art.

The earliest records indicate that Maison Pinat of France was recognized for manufacturing chocolate molds by hand in 1820 and Maison Cadot followed in 1826, making molds of pewter for chocolate and ice cream.

In 1832, Jean-Baptiste Létang started selling chocolate molds to chocolate makers. There were two Létang companies: Létang Fils and Létang Marie, the latter established in 1855. The French companies began producing chocolate molds featuring ornate shapes, national monuments, everyday objects, people, and animals.

The German company of Hermann Walter started production of molds in 1866 with Anton Reiche, another German firm, opening in 1870. Additional chocolate mold manufacturers are listed in the chart on page 7 of this book.

The labor that went into making just one mold was considerable. The process of crafting a wonderfully detailed, molded piece of chocolate was very time-consuming and required meticulous work.

First, artists would sketch designs for chocolate molds and then sculpt the figure out of a plaster-like material—not much different from the work of the Renaissance sculptors. The facial detail on many chocolate molds, especially the Santa molds, is brilliant, comparable to those sculpted by Donatello and Michelangelo.

Face of Santa,
Anton Reiche.

The artists who designed chocolate molds went nameless, however, and were never acknowledged, except for the mysterious "FQ" who worked for Létang and signed his initials on several of his designs.

When finished, the sculpted piece was cut in half. The two pieces were then pressed into sand and removed, leaving an impression into which molten metal could be poured to make a casting or "die." The finished metal castings were then placed onto presses that used up to 250 tons of pressure to stamp the original designs into sheets of tin. The heavier presses were needed to ensure that the new molds would show their intricate details.

The newly stamped works of art were trimmed and marked with the company name, logo, and design number.

Imagine the amount of effort needed to delight a child who would hold his molded chocolate bunny for just a few seconds before biting the ears off.

Many French chocolatiers preferred the German designed molds because of their diverse selection and extraordinary detail. Before long, the respected French mold makers were in strong competition with German companies such as Hermann Walter, Laurösch,

Kutzscher, and of course Anton Reiche. The Anton Reiche factory alone had thousands of employees at the height of its production in the 1920s, and produced at least fifty thousand extremely detailed designs.

In the United States, starting about 1880, Eppelsheimer, Jaburg, The American Chocolate Mould Co., and Allmetal Chocolate Mold Co. were producing metal chocolate molds.

Chocolate molds have been made of many materials, including pewter, lead, copper, nickel, and tinned steel. Plastic molds were mass-produced in the 1960s, and since plastic was less expensive to produce and easier to work with for mold making and chocolate molding, the metal chocolate molds became less desirable. As metal chocolate mold factories went out of business, many of the molds were recycled or scrapped.

Létang Fils, Matfer, and The American Chocolate Mould Company are continuing to produce a limited line of metal chocolate molds today.

Chalkware Santas, crafted from chocolate molds, at Vaillancourt Folk Art Studios.

Christmas ornaments in chocolate, by Robert Twardzik.
Photo by Marcus Pinto.

Antique chocolate molds are still in use today and not only for molding chocolate. Artists are drawn to these molds for their historic significance and also for the whimsical quality they bring to the artist's work. The wonderful detail of mold designs and the many themes to choose from make them desirable for alternate uses such as papier mâché, chalkware, beeswax, soap, and hard candy.

The appeal of these historic objects is truly standing the test of time. Antique chocolate molds bring a sense of nostalgia and pleasure to the collector. Collecting them is an exciting and unpredictable hobby, as you never know when or where you will find another marvelous mold! With so many designs available, the collector will probably never encounter all of them.

Chocolate Mold Manufacturers

Overview

The following is a selection from a comprehensive chart available exclusively from Carolyn Byrnes. This information has been assembled as a reference for identifying the origin and age of molds by recognizing their stampings.

The complete chart covers over one hundred different marks, both manufacturers and distributors. This tool is useful in understanding your mold collection and is based upon information accumulated from several sources including *The Chocolate Mould,* by Henry and Laure Dorchy.

Following the chart are photographs of the marks used by the manufacturers listed, as well as brief historical background on three of the companies. While this book is not intended to provide detailed information on all of the companies that manufactured molds, I have highlighted three that I felt would be especially interesting. More detailed information about the manufacturers' history can be found in the Dorchy book.

Company	Country of origin	Dates	Distributors other than manufacturer
Létang	Paris, France	1832-1998	Dunan, Smeulders
Walter	Berlin, Germany	1866-1970	Bonck, Cerfontaine, Cluydts, Nieulant-Pelkman, Pettavel, Smeulders, Van Emden
Anton Reiche	Dresden, Germany	1870-1972	Hans Bruham, Hans Bruhn, DeHaeck-Delbaere, Diltoer, Dunan, Eppelsheimer, May Frhes, Monos, Schultz, Sondaar, Vetrerer, Weygandt, Winkler
Laurösch	Esslingen Schwäbish-Gmünd, Germany	1875-1966	Nieulant-Pelkman
Eppelsheimer	New York, U.S.A.	1880-1947	Bought by American Chocolate Mould Company
Jaburg	New York, U.S.A.	1885-1951	Thomas Mills
Sommet	Paris, France	1888-1962	Nieulant-Pelkman, Smeulders (bought Trottier, sold to Matfer)
Kutzscher	Schwarzenberg, Germany	1900-1929	H.Schuenemann in New York
Heris	Nurnberg, Germany	1900-1963	Oosterbaan & Zn., Winkler
Riecke	Dresden, Germany; Bergisch-Gladbach, Germany; Wallbach Sackingnen, Germany; and Helmond, Holland	1900-1970s	Nieulant-Pelkman, Pettavel, Vormenfabriek
Henri LeCerf	Cologne, Germany	1905-1971	
Teich	Vienna, Austria	1911-1965	
Vormenfabriek	Tilburg, Holland	1921-1972	Boyen, Cluydts, Darchambeau, DeLille, J.K.V., Waldek, Zeist (bought some Riecke equipment, bought by American Chocolate Mould Company)
Allmetal	New York, U.S.A.	1946-Present	None
Weygandt	New York, U.S.A.	1947-1968	None
Hörnlein	Hamburg, Germany	1950s-1980	Hahn in the US and J.K.V. in Europe (bought Bruham, Bruhn and Laurösch)

Anton Reiche: An Entrepreneur

I have been extremely privileged to make the acquaintance of a great-granddaughter of Anton Reiche, Monica Tinhofer, who provided much of the information used in the next two sections. I hope the memories she has so generously shared of the Reiche family will be as much a treasure for you as they have been for me.

Anton Reiche was born in Wilsdruff, Germany near Dresden in 1845 and was the youngest of six children. He came from a farming family whose heritage could be traced back to their knightly ancestry in 1495.

Grandson Carl Reiche and family in front of the house where Anton Reiche was born. The house was torn down shortly after the photo was taken. *Photo courtesy of great-granddaughter Rita Reiche.*

When Anton was young, his master—a man by the name of Hoyer—insisted that he learn the trade of working with sheet metal. He therefore traveled during 1867-1870 to France, where he apprenticed in the art of making chocolate molds at the House of Létang in Paris.

In September of 1870, Dresden had become a boomtown and Anton Reiche opened a workshop for metals. Thanks to industrial development, metal workers were seeing large profits.

Also during this time, the ingredients for making chocolate were becoming less expensive and were more available to everyone. In the middle of the nineteenth century the chocolate industry was reigning throughout Europe and the rest of the world. Anton Reiche saw the value in this market and, as a result, decided to manufacture chocolate molds.

Instead of using the acetate susceptible and potentially toxic copper materials then currently in use for making chocolate molds, Anton Reiche invented a specially coated tin for use with his molds and used up to twenty tons per day. His chocolate molds became highly sought after, not only in Germany but throughout the world. During his first few years in business, he expanded significantly and by 1902 the company had 876 em-

ployees. Reiche soon became the largest mold manufacturer in the world and won many awards for his quality workmanship.

In addition to producing chocolate molds, the factory, located in Bambergerstraße, Germany, made printed tin posters, printed and lacquered tin boxes, tin trays, children's tin toys, and the actual machines used for the production of chocolate and candy.

Ruler made by the Anton Reiche Company.

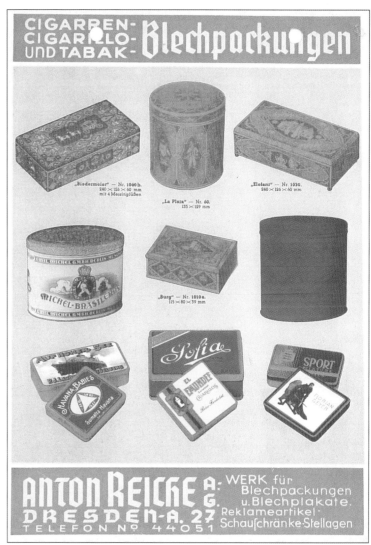

Ad showing tin boxes manufactured at the Anton Reiche factory. *Photo courtesy of Rita Reiche.*

Very rare tin tray, also made by the Anton Reiche factory.
The tray is 13-1/2" in diameter and is marked Anton Reiche.

Anton Reiche was known to work extremely long hours in his workshop inventing machines for making and selling chocolate. He invented the "Schokolade Automat" for the Stollwercks chocolate company, which automatically dispensed chocolate bars.

Huge Stollwerck's chocolate bar mold, 20" x 11", ca.1920.

Anton Reiche died in 1913 at the age of sixty-eight, leaving his wife and nine children. He was remembered by his family for his humanity, kindheartedness, and industrious dedication to his chocolate mold empire. His three sons, Max, Anton, and Alfred, were left to run an industry that was unrivaled by any other chocolate mold company in the world.

Great-granddaughters Rita and Audrey Reiche are the daughters of Anton Reiche's grandson, Carl Reiche. They described to me the idyllic life led by the family near the beautiful apple orchards outside of Dresden, and the wonderful and loving childhood of Carl and his brother Hans. However, this peaceful existence came to an abrupt end when Carl was just fifteen years old, as World War II began.

The Anton Reiche factory offered 50,000 different designs of chocolate molds. These designs were illustrated in the now famous and rare Anton Reiche catalogues, which were also the calling cards for the company at the time and served as effective advertising tools.

When customers entered the showroom at the factory they felt more like they had walked into a museum because the molds were so artfully displayed.

Front and back covers of Anton Reiche catalog.

Tragedy struck the family in many ways. The first of many losses was when the Nazis took over the Anton Reiche factory in the late 1930s and began manufacturing Nazi memorabilia, including Nazi chocolate molds.

The most tragic blow to the Anton Reiche family, however, was the death of Anne Reiche, wife of Anton Reiche Jr. and mother of Carl, at the concentration camp in Ravensbruck. Carl Reiche, along with his mother and father, was jailed by the Nazis for five months. Carl and his father were released; their beloved Anne, however, was deported to the concentration camp where she died.

The Anton Reiche famly was extremely grateful for the allied bombing of Dresden, which helped to end the war, even though it meant a huge loss of the family's fortunes. The great empire of Anton Reiche was destroyed during the night bombings of February 1945. Thousands of molds were scattered throughout the factory ruins and were disregarded as survivors fled for their lives. All that remained of the factory was one building and a few catalogues that had been thoughtfully placed in a safe.

The only building from the original Anton Reiche factory still standing. *Photo courtesy of Rita Reiche.*

Despite the devastation left by the war, the brothers Reiche were able to pull the company out of its ruins by June of 1950—in time to celebrate the firm's 80th anniversary. The factory remained in operation and was producing molds until its close in 1972.

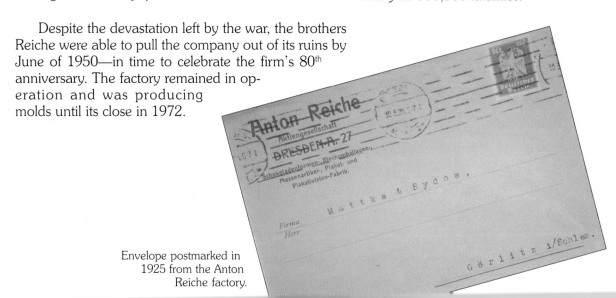

Envelope postmarked in 1925 from the Anton Reiche factory.

Monica Tinhofer: Memories of the Anton Reiche Family

Monica Tinhofer, the great-granddaughter of Anton Reiche, was born in Dresden in 1928. Although her parents subsequently moved to Vienna, Austria, Monica spent summers and school holidays at her grandparents' home in Dresden. Due to the threat of wartime violence and bombings, Monica was sent back to Dresden as everyone felt Dresden would be spared any bombing because it was a cultural center and couldn't possibly be considered a target.

However, the world saw Dresden as a threat. On February 13 and 14 of 1945, the Allied Forces bombed Dresden relentlessly. Monica remembers being sixteen years old at the time. Her grandfather, Rudolph (who was a connoisseur of fine wines), hurried Monica and her grandmother Maria (daughter of Anton Reiche) past the basement and down into his wine cellar, where they waited, praying to survive the destruction happening above them.

After several days had passed, Maria and Rudolph looked out. Choking on the smoke-filled air, they were horrified to see that Dresden was literally flattened—completely ruined.

They took Monica up the hill to the only house standing in the area—her uncle's home. As surviving family members gathered, they realized that Ella, one of Anton Reiche's daughters, had perished during the bombing.

Monica's grandfather had operated a hospital where all of the patients had been killed during the bombing, as had most of their neighbors and friends. At sixteen, Monica was faced with the grim reality that many of her classmates had been killed as well.

The horrendous consequence of the bombing resulted in 50,000 dead and wounded in Dresden alone—although, according to German reports there were as many as 300,000 fatalities.

The family went to the Anton Reiche factory. Only one small building was left standing—the rest had been devastated.

Monica says she remembers seeing the chocolate molds scattered all over the ground. There was no time to salvage them as everyone was unsure about the days ahead—would there be more bombings? What would happen to them as survivors?

All of the Anton Reiche children had lost their substantial fortunes as quickly as the bombs were dropped.

Monica was determined to get home to Vienna and let her parents know she was living. She set out alone from Dresden to Vienna with nothing but a stale loaf of bread. She walked most of the way, although sometimes army trucks would give her rides. Monica slept in ditches, always fearful for her life yet resolute that she would make it home. She finally made it to Vienna after four days and went straight to her mother's dress shop. Her mother fainted when she saw her walk through the door—she couldn't believe her daughter was alive and standing right in front of her.

Monica returned to the Anton Reiche factory with her husband after the Berlin wall came down in 1990. Several family members met there and solemnly divided the few rescued treasures from the former Anton Reiche empire. To this day, Monica has retained rare master catalogues and old ledgers from the company, as well as the photo album Anton Reiche had commissioned showing every room in the factory.

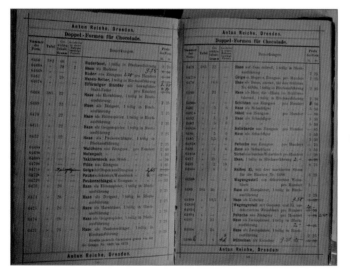

Old Anton Reiche company ledger. *Collection of Monica Tinhofer.*

Monica's childhood memories of the holidays include her grandmother gathering the family around the piano to sing Christmas carols. Monica said she always had a hard time concentrating on the singing, because she could see all the molded chocolate figures sent to the family by Anton Reiche customers placed on the table. Monica said she really just wanted to eat some of the

chocolate before her grandmother had it sent to children's homes and hospitals.

Growing up around the largest chocolate mold manufactory in the world was always exciting for Monica. She recalls the showrooms for the chocolate molds as being absolutely beautiful. Thinking back, she notes that she never wanted a chocolate mold as a child, just the chocolate. At the time, of course, she could have had any mold she wanted from the factory store, but never acquired even one to start her collection.

Girl with rabbit, Anton Reiche #24889, 5", ca.1920. *Collection of Monica Tinhofer.* $300-$400.

Monica has spent years collecting documents, photos, and chocolate molds from the Anton Reiche factory. She co-authored the book *Osterhase, Nikolaus & Zeppelin*, which shows chocolate molds and old catalogue pages along with a great deal of Anton Reiche history. She also orchestrated an exhibition in Vienna on chocolate molds a few years ago and people from many countries sent molds for the display.

Monica's dream to open a chocolate mold museum will come to pass at the German Castle Rammenau in the summer of 2005.

Weygandt

In 1935, the T. C. Weygandt Company, located in New York City, signed an exclusive contract with Anton Reiche to distribute Reiche chocolate molds in the United States. The contract, noting transfer of the patent for a "useful mold for the manufacture of chocolate articles," was signed by Anton Reiche's sons Anton and Max and stamped by the American Consulate's Office in Dresden.

Max turned the business to "warwork," which included marked depth charge triggers and end covers. In 1947, the Weygandt Company started manufacturing their own chocolate mold designs; however they went bankrupt in 1968. At that time, the Kaderli family moved the company to their home in Old Greenwich, Connecticut.

Max Kaderli founded Emkay that same year, and began operating as both a manufacturer and distributor of chocolate molds. Emkay had a gentleman's agreement with the American Chocolate Mould Company (ACMC) that Emkay (Weygandt) would distribute hollow chocolate molds made by Vormenfabriek while ACMC would distribute only the Vormenfabriek flat molds. In addition to chocolate molds, Emkay began supplying a variety of confectionery machinery.

Currently, Emkay Confectionery Machinery sells polycarbonate chocolate molds as well as a variety of production and processing equipment for the confectionery industry.

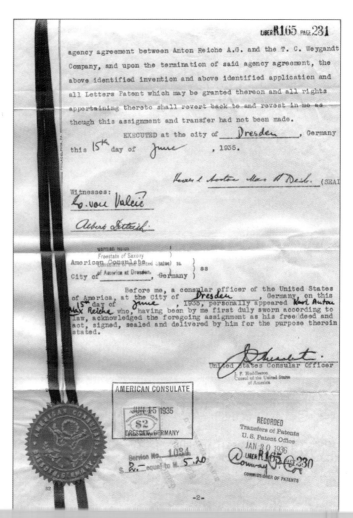

Courtesy of Emkay Confectionery Machinery.

A few years later, in the late 1930s, Max Kaderli came to New York from Switzerland speaking six languages and began work as a foreign language secretary for Weygandt. In 1940, Max and his wife bought the company from its German owners when it was facing bankruptcy due to sanctions enacted in 1939 that prevented importation of the chocolate molds from Germany.

Allmetal Chocolate
Mold Company is All American

The following history was graciously provided by the Micelli Chocolate Mold Company.

It was 1918 when Joseph Micelli Sr. brought his metal fabrication expertise to the Eppelsheimer mold manufacturing company of New York City.

Joseph stayed with the company through its change to Warren Brothers as a plant supervisor until about 1941, the onset of World War II. During the war, Joseph worked for the US Navy as a ship builder; his primary work was fabricating battleships including the USS *Wisconsin*.

In August 1946, Joseph Micelli Sr. and his son Ned founded the ALLMETAL CHOCOLATE MOLD COMPANY in New York City.

The family company manufactured and repaired metal chocolate molds for themselves and for several other well-known mold manufacturers. For this reason, Allmetal did not stamp their name on the molds they made.

This American mold manufacturing company quickly became known throughout the confectionery industry for their high quality chocolate molds, which earned the nickname "shockproof" due to their enhanced working strength.

From 1946 through the early 1980s, The Allmetal Chocolate Mold Co. produced over 2000 different designs of metal chocolate molds. Many of the mold designs were Allmetal originals hand sculpted by Ned and his brother-in-law Peter Sceri. Ned is an expert in chocolate molding and was the initiator of the "pack on the back" on the traditional standing rabbits. Chocolate makers were having ear breakage problems with the standard design for the traditional standing rabbit because the ears tilted back and would easily break off when the chocolate contracted.

Ned and his father Joseph, having an extensive knowledge of shrinkage effects from decades in foundry work, corrected the problem by joining the ears to the basket, therefore allowing the chocolate to shrink without breaking. This worked so well they used the design for dozens and dozens of applications. Ned did all the redesigns and engraving with his own hands then, and is still active in the business today.

In 1956, the Micelli family opened the second Allmetal manufacturing plant in New York City, and by the late 1960s Ned had pioneered the use of thermoform plastic molds for chocolate in the U.S.A.

By the 1970s, the remaining U.S. based metal chocolate mold manufacturers had closed or were closing their manufacturing businesses and began importing metal and plastic molds from Europe.

At around that same time, Allmetal began manufacturing polycarbonate plastic injection molds while continuing to make metal molds.

Allmetal was at this point the only U.S. company left manufacturing industrial chocolate molds in the United States.

In 1975, Ned's oldest son Joe joined the company and expanded the plastic injection molding and tooling operations. Joseph Sr. continued the family tradition of hand crafting metal chocolate molds up until about a week before he passed away in 1979.

The early 1980s signaled the end of the metal chocolate mold era.

In 1985, Ned's son John joined the company and was able to assist with die manufacturing. John also introduced computer-aided design and manufacturing technology to the company. A few years later, Ned's daughter Theresa joined the family business, focusing on accounting and running the busy office.

In 1991, the company changed its name from Allmetal Chocolate Mold Company to Micelli Chocolate Mold Company, as the majority of their manufacturing had gone to polycarbonate chocolate molds.

Allmetal Chocolate Mold Company continued to produce metal chocolate molds for one of their loyal customers until 1998.

Today, Micelli Chocolate Mold Company is the largest manufacturer of chocolate molds in North America and is the only North American based manufacturer of injection polycarbonate chocolate molds.

Shown here are just a few of the metal chocolate molds that the Allmetal Chocolate Mold Company manufactured. The molds shown are in various stages of production; note the unfinished flanges on some of them. I am sure you will recognize many of these mold designs and be pleasantly surprised to find out that they were manufactured by the Allmetal Chocolate Mold Company. All molds and catalogs shown here are courtesy of the Micelli family.

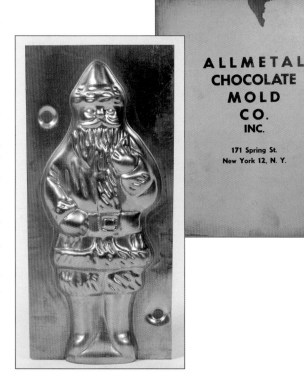

ALLMETAL
CHOCOLATE
MOLD
CO.
INC.

171 Spring St.
New York 12, N. Y.

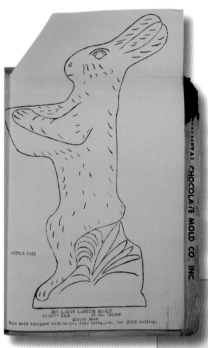

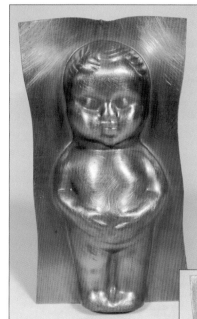

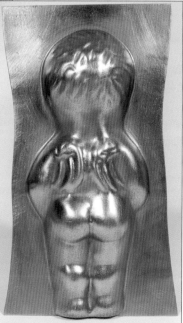

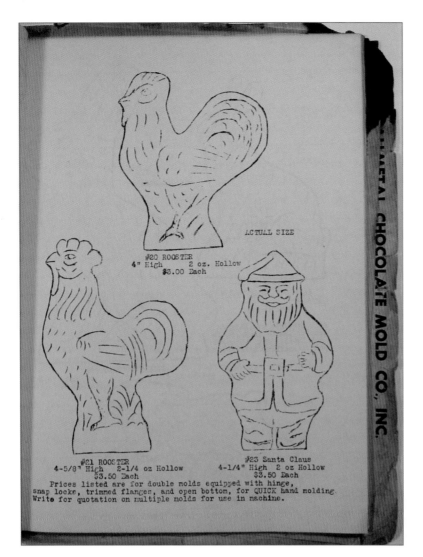

ACTUAL SIZE

#20 ROOSTER
4" High   2 oz. Hollow
$3.00 Each

#21 ROOSTER
4-5/8" High   2-1/4 oz Hollow
$3.50 Each

#23 Santa Claus
4-1/4" High   2 oz Hollow
$3.50 Each

Prices listed are for double molds equipped with hinge,
snap locks, trimmed flanges, and open bottom, for QUICK hand molding.
Write for quotation on multiple molds for use in machine.

ALLMETAL CHOCOLATE MOLD CO., INC.

All Eyes On....

ANALYSES OF THE
RAW MATERIAL
ENSURES
UNVARYING QUALITY

TEST STAMPINGS
ENSURE
SUITABILITY OF
METAL

FINISHED MOLDS
ARE TESTED
FOR STRENGTH OF
SOLDERING

COMPLETED MOLDS
ARE EXAMINED
BEFORE
SHIPPING

Allmetal
CHOCOLATE MOLD CO., INC.
171 SPRING STREET   NEW YORK 12, NEW YORK
WOrth 2-0934.

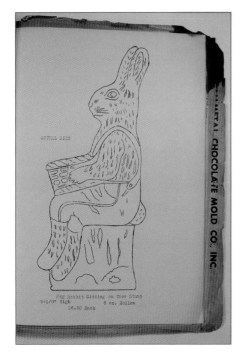

ACTUAL SIZE

#48 Rabbit Sitting on Tree Stump
9-1/2" High   8 oz. Hollow
        $6.50 Each

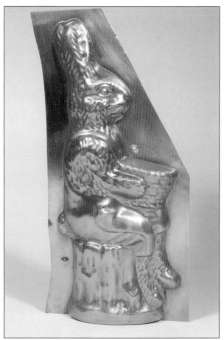

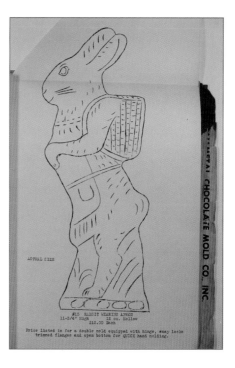

ACTUAL SIZE

#15 RABBIT WEARING APRON
11-3/4" High   12 oz. Hollow
        $12.00 Each
Price listed is for a double mold equipped with hinge, snap locks,
trimmed flanges and open bottom for QUICK hand molding.

Master die photo courtesy of John Micelli.

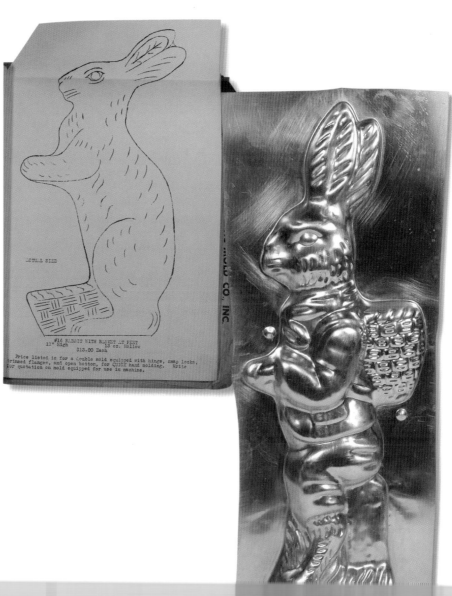

ACTUAL SIZE

#16 RABBIT WITH BASKET AT FEET
11" High   13 oz. Hollow
        $13.00 Each
Price listed is for a double mold equipped with hinge, snap locks,
trimmed flanges, and open bottom, for QUICK hand molding. Write
for quotation on mold equipped for use in machine.

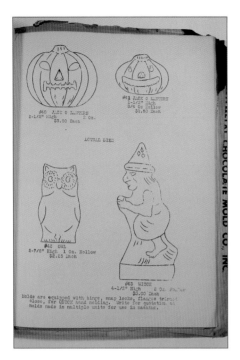

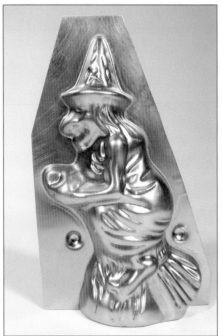

Master die photo courtesy
of John Micelli.

Master die photo Courtesy
of John Micelli.

18

The Molds

Bunnies

The ancient Saxons celebrated the return of spring with their festival "Eastre." The goddess Eastre was worshipped by the Anglo-Saxons through her earthly symbol, the rabbit.

Side view of mold and chalkware.

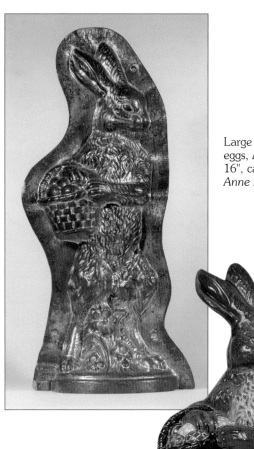

Large Bunny with basket of eggs, Anton Reiche #17438, 16", ca.1920. *Collection of Anne Launius.* $3,000 and up.

Chalkware by Anne Launius.

Page from Anton Reiche catalog.

Washer bunny, Anton Reiche #28331, 5", ca.1930. *Collection of Kathryn Campbell.* $200-$300.

Chalkware by Kathryn Campbell.

Chalkware by Kathryn Campbell.

Reverse side of mold.

20

Small washerwoman bunny, Anton Reiche #6424, 3-1/2", ca.1910. $250.

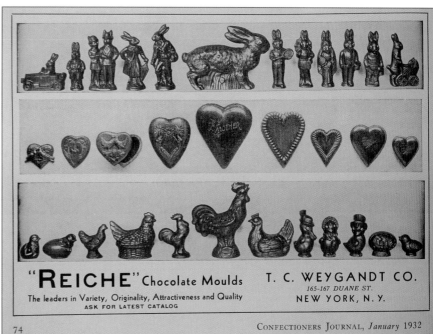

Advertisement for Anton Reiche chocolate molds.

Larger washerwoman bunny, Anton Reiche #6801, 5-1/4",/ca.1910. $250.

Mother pushing baby in carriage, Anton Reiche #17762, 6", ca.1920. *Collection of Diane Cazalet.* $250-$400,

Mother pushing empty carriage, Teich #3718, 5-1/4", ca.1930. $150-$250.

Bunny with cornucopia on back, Anton Reiche, 4", ca. 1920. $250-$350.

Chalkware and photo by Vaillancourt Folk Art.

Peasant dress bunny, Kutzscher #5591, ca.1920. *Collection and photo courtesy of Vaillancourt.* $250-$400.

Page from Kutzscher catalog.

22

Chalkware by Anne Launius.

Bunny with Cornucopia filled with eggs, #5752, 4-3/4", ca.1930. *Collection of Anne Launius.* $250-$400.

Page from Laurösch catalog.

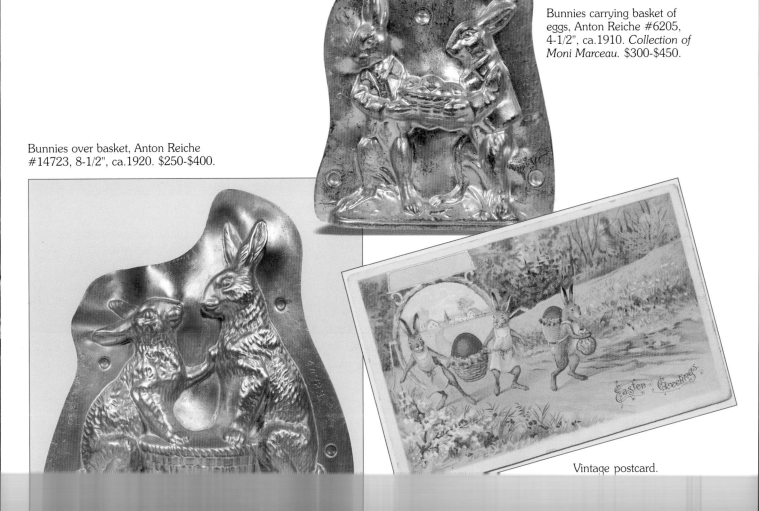

Bunnies carrying basket of eggs, Anton Reiche #6205, 4-1/2", ca.1910. *Collection of Moni Marceau.* $300-$450.

Bunnies over basket, Anton Reiche #14723, 8-1/2", ca.1920. $250-$400.

Vintage postcard.

Chocolate by Morgen Chocolate.

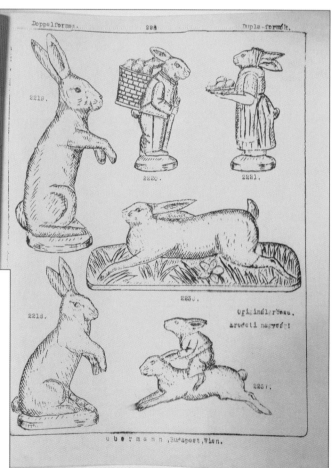

Bunny with basket of eggs on back,
Walter #8486, 5", ca.1930. $250.

Bunnies with eggs, Walter #8492, 5-1/2", ca.1920.
Collection of Morgen Chocolate. $250-$350.

Dressed bunny with
walking stick and basket,
Obermann 3-1/2",ca.1920.
$250.

Page from Obermann catalog.

24

Chalkware by Carolyn Deschenes.

Butler bunny in checkered pants, 15-1/2", ca.1920. $2,000 and up.

Dressed bunny with walking stick and basket. *Collection of Carolyn Deschenes.* $250.

Chocolate by Lynea Lefler-Harrison of Calico Chocolates.

Bunny with apron, Anton Reiche #6758, 4-1/4", ca.1910. $150.

Beautiful bunny face. *Collection of Diane Cazalet.*

Paws for bunny.

Diane Cazalet's molds on display at the Copia Museum in Napa, California.

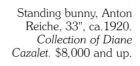

Standing bunny, Anton Reiche, 33", ca.1920. *Collection of Diane Cazalet.* $8,000 and up.

Bunny carrying yoked baskets, Kutzscher #13089, 8", ca.1920. *Collection of Anne Launius.* $350-$450.

Page from Kutzscher catalog.

Reverse.

Reverse.

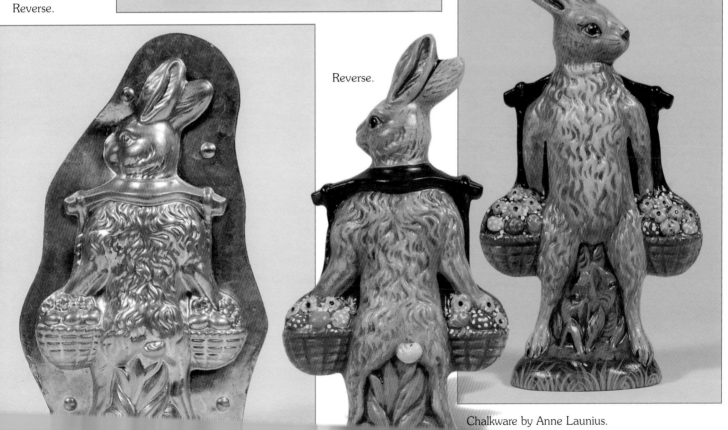

Chalkware by Anne Launius.

Weygandt advertisement.

Upright walking bunny,
Weygandt, 22", ca.1940.
*Collection of Ginny
Betourne.* $500 and up.

Papier mâché by Ginny
Betourne.

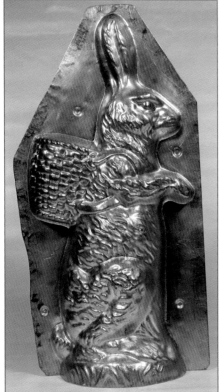

Large bunny with basket, Eppelsheimer
#8046, 14-1/2", ca.1920. $500.

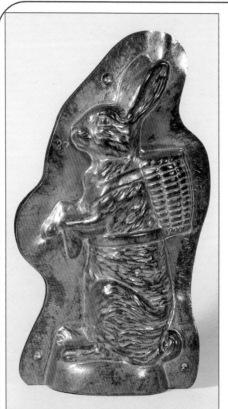

Classic bunny with basket, Anton
Reiche #6746, 9", ca.1910. $250.

Chocolate by Morgen Chocolate.

28

Weygandt advertisement.

Chocolate by Lynea Lefler-
Harrison of Calico Chocolates.

Large bunny with basket,
Weygandt #236, 18",
ca.1920. $800 and up.

Boy with chocolate bunnies, ca.1920.

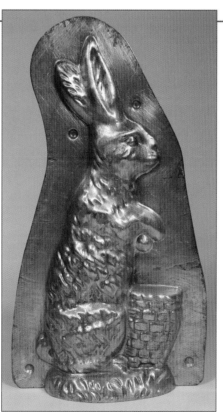

Bunny with basket, Heris #4155, 9",
ca.1930. $150-$200.

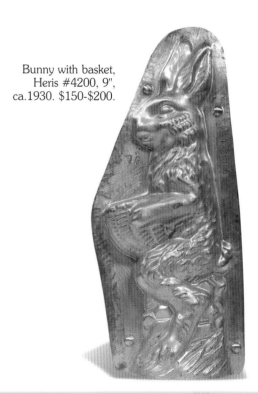

Bunny with basket,
Heris #4200, 9",
ca.1930. $150-$200.

Startled "Velveteen Rabbit" with
basket, Laurösch #3072, 12-1/2",
ca.1930. $250.

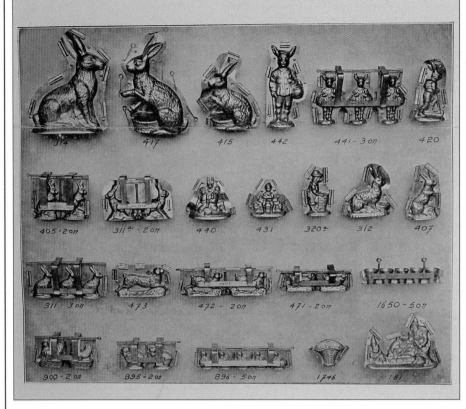

NEW EASTER LINE 1929.

Karl Pauli advertisement for chocolate molds.

Bunny with basket, Laurösch #4033,
ca.1930. *Collection of Ginny
Betourne.* $250.

Papier mâché by Ginny Betourne
of Trout Creek Folk Art.

Papier mâché by
Ginny Betourne.

Page from an Anton
Reiche catalog.
*Collection of Monica
Tinhofer.*

Weygandt catalog page.

Startled bunny,
Eppelsheimer #8238,
13-1/2", ca.1930.
*Collection of Ginny
Betourne.* $250-$450.

Four piece rabbit, #3956, ca.1920.
Collection of Monica Tinhofer. $350-$450.

Sitting bunny made to hold egg, Anton
Reiche #6203, 11", ca.1920. $350-$450.

Additional view.

Reverse.

Close up of gorgeous face detail.

Bunny with basket, Eppelsheimer
#6629, 12-1/2", ca.1920. *Papier mâché
work and mold, collection of Ginny
Betourne.* $350-$450.

Mold display at Diane Cazalet show.

Begging bunny, Anton
Reiche, #6204, 11-1/2",
ca.1910. $250.

Bunny with paws
on basket, Anton
Reiche, 8",
ca.1920. $250.

Bunny with basket, Laurösch #3014, 6", ca.1920. $250.

"Mrs. Rabbit Loves Chocolate," papier mâché by Debbee Thibault. Photo by Carolyn Clark.

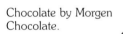

Chocolate by Morgen Chocolate.

Additional view.

Begging bunny, Eppelsheimer #4603, 9-1/2", ca.1920. $150-$250.

Mini bunny sitting up, Anton Reiche #6307, 3-1/2", ca.1920. $150.

Mini upright bunny, Laurösch #3004, 3-1/2", ca.1920. $150.

Five bunnies in a row, Eppelsheimer #8042, 11", ca.1930. $150.

Yellow ware by Kathryn Campbell.

Walking bunny, T C Weygandt #25513, 9", ca.1920. *Collection of Rex Morgen.* $450 and up.

Standing bunny, Anton Reiche, 20", ca.1920. *Collection of Moni Marceau.* $4,000 and up.

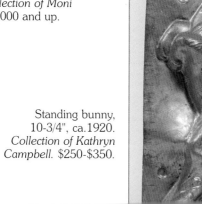

Standing bunny, 10-3/4", ca.1920. *Collection of Kathryn Campbell.* $250-$350.

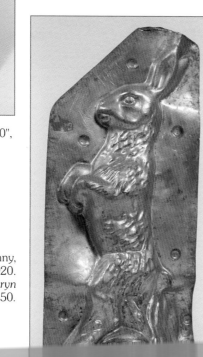

Walking bunny, Anton Reiche #14702, 8", ca.1920. $400-$650.

Running bunny, Anton Reiche #6264, 10", ca.1900. $500 and up.

Walking bunny, Anton Reiche #14701, 12-3/4", ca.1920. *Collection of Kathryn Campbell.* $1,000 and up.

Yellow ware walking bunny by Kathryn Campbell.

Small walking bunny, Teich #305, 4-3/4", ca.1920. $150.

Large running bunny, Anton Reiche #26959, 18-3/4", marked "Yeostros," ca.1920. $4,000 and up.

Beeswax figure by Kathryn Campbell.

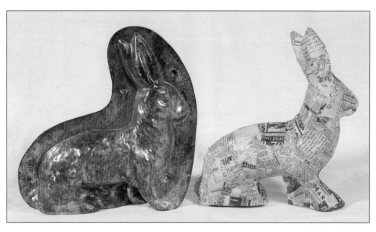

Papier mâché bunny and mold. *Collection of Ginny Betourne.*

Large bunny, "Made in Berlin," 12", ca.1920.
$350-$500.

"Mrs. Bunny Rabbit," Limited Edition by
~~Robbon Thibault. Photo by Caroline Clark.~~

Sitting "Velveteen Rabbit," Laurösch
~~#3071, 11", ca.1930. $250.~~

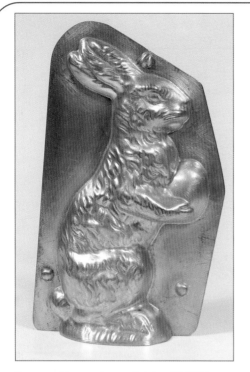

Bunny with egg, Anton Reiche #26997,
7-3/4", ca.1930. $175-$250.

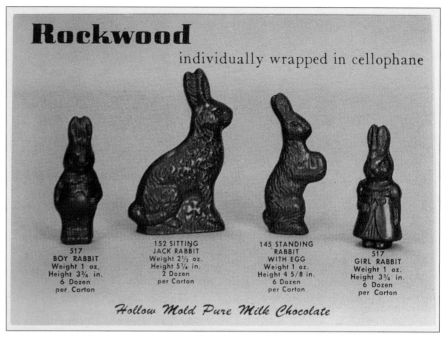

Rockwood chocolate bunnies advertisement.

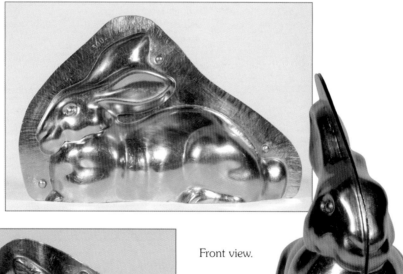

Laying bunny,
Laurösch #300,
9", ca.1950.
$250.

Front view.

Bunny holding egg, Laurösch
#3014, ca.1940. $250.

Startled bunny, Laurösch
#3040, 10-1/2", ca.1930.
$200-$250.

Girl with chocolate bunny
in cone, ca.1920.

Chocolate by Morgen Chocolate.

Bunny pulling basket, Heris #4196,
6-1/2", ca.1930. $350-$450.

Bunny with egg on back, Walter
#2639, 8", ca.1920. $250.

Chocolate by Morgen Chocolate.

Page from Heris catalog.

Chalkware by Kathi Bejma of Walnut Ridge Classics.

Multi-piece rabbit with wheelbarrow, Eppelsheimer #6351, 9", ca.1930. *Collection of Rex Morgen.* $500-$750.

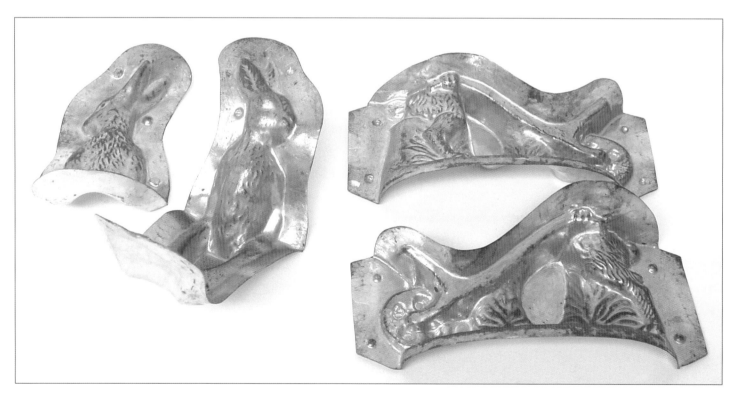

Piece detail.

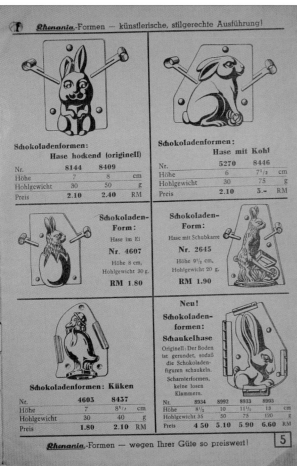

Schokoladenformen:
Hase hockend (originell)

Nr.	8144	8409	
Höhe	7	8	cm
Hohlgewicht	30	50	g
Preis	2.10	2.40	RM

Schokoladenformen:
Hase mit Kohl

Nr.	5270	8446	
Höhe	6	7½	cm
Hohlgewicht	30	75	g
Preis	2.10	5.—	RM

Schokoladen-
Form:
Hase im Ei
Nr. 4607
Höhe 8 cm,
Hohlgewicht 30 g.
RM 1.80

Schokoladen-
Form:
Hase mit Schubkarre
Nr. 2645
Höhe 9½ cm,
Hohlgewicht 20 g.
RM 1.90

Schokoladenformen: Küken

Nr.	4603	8437	
Höhe	7	8½	cm
Hohlgewicht	30	40	g
Preis	1.80	2.10	RM

Neu!
Schokoladen-
formen:
Schaukelhase
Originell: Der Boden
ist gerundet, sodaß
die Schokoladen-
figuren schaukeln.
Scharnierformen,
keine losen
Klammern.

Nr.	8934	8992	8933	8993	
Höhe	8½	10	11½	13	cm
Hohlgewicht	35	50	75	120	g
Preis	4.50	5.10	5.90	6.60	RM

5

Ostern 1938

Lamm-Backformen
Kräftige Ausführung.
Figur schön und deutlich geprägt!

Nr. 4302. ¼ Liter, 8½ cm hoch, 10½ cm lang, RM 0.80
„ 4305. ½ „ 11 „ „ 14 „ „ „ 1.05
„ 4510. 1 „ 15 „ „ 20 „ „ „ 1.60
(Rezepte siehe Seite 2)

Müller
Vertretungen
Nordhausen
Steinstraße 33

Reiner Fischer
Köln 44
Maximinenstraße 10 - 20, hinter dem Hauptbahnhof — Parkplatz am Hause.
Ruf 75182

Rhenania Konditorei-Maschinen und Einrichtungen

Gegründet 1902

Pages from 1938 Reiner Fischer catalog.

Bunny pushing wheelbarrow, Walter #2645, 4", ca.1920. $125.

Twisted sticks of barley sugar were originally made in the seventeenth century by boiling down refined cane sugar (a new product at that time) with barley water, cream of tartar, and water. During the eighteenth century, metal molds were used to create the wonderful variety of shapes known as Barley Sugar Clear Toys. These became a popular Victorian Christmas treat.

Vintage postcard.

Barley candy by Dorothy Timberlake Candies.

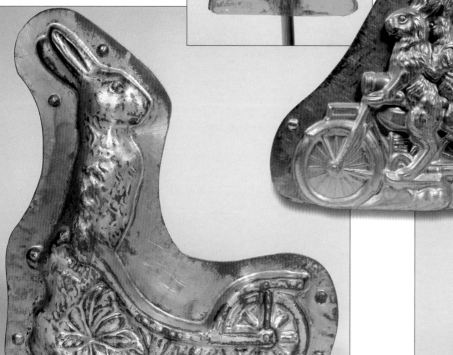

Family ride, Walter #5307, 6", ca.1920. $450.

Bunny pushing wheelbarrow, Anton Reiche #13274, 7-1/4", ca.1920. $350 and up.

Reverse.

Chalkware by Penny Burns.

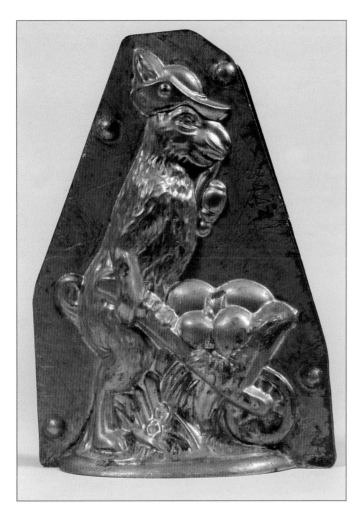

Bunny with pipe pushing wheelbarrow,
Walter #8444, 5 3/4", ca 1920, $250.

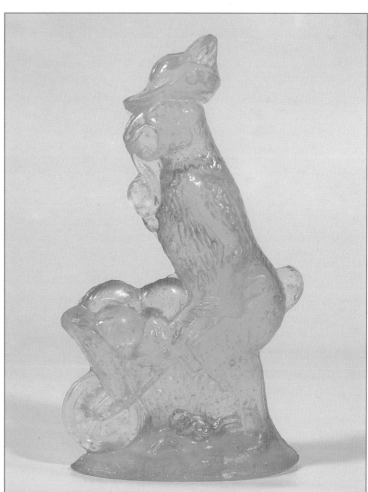

Barley candy by Dorothy Timberlake Candies.

Bunnies riding motorcycle, Anton Reiche #21887, 4", ca.1920. $250.

Bunny riding bicycle, Anton Reiche #6385, 5-1/2", ca.1920. *Collection of Moni Marceau.* $450.

Chocolate by Morgen Chocolate.

Bunny on bicycle, Anton Reiche #6387, ca.1910. *Collection and photo courtesy of Erwin and Monika Gschwind.* $450.

Drawing from an Anton Reiche catalog.

Barley candy by Dorothy Timberlake Candies.

Page from Heris catalog.

Bunny on scooter, #420, 7",
ca.1920. $250-$350.

Bunny driving cargo hauler, Heris #4194, 6", ca.1940. $250.

Bunny riding in car, Laurösch #3052, 4-1/2", ca.1930. $250.

Vintage photo of girl at Easter.

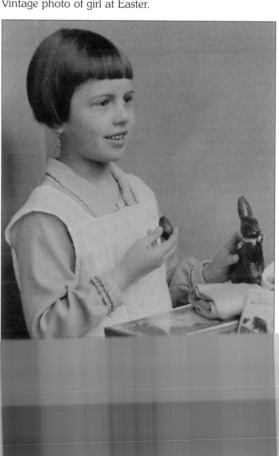

Chick pulling bunny in egg chariot, Laurösch #3055, 5", ca.1920. *Collection of Rex Morgen.* $200-$300.

Bunny riding rocket, #3165, 7", ca.1960. $250.

Rooster pulling bunny, Walter, 10", ca.1920. *Collection of Ginny Betourne.* $450-$650.

Bunny pulling wagon, Heris #4085, 6", ca.1930. $150-$200.

Bunny in chariot, 7", ca.1930. *Collection of Monica Tinhofer.* $350-$450.

Bunny and chick hatching from egg, Made in Germany #375, 5-1/2", ca.1930. *Collection of Kathryn Campbell.* $250.

Chalkware with "onion skin" finish (Russian tradition) by Kathryn Campbell.

Papier mâché inspired by a chocolate mold, created by Susan Brack.

Page from Anton Reiche catalog. *Collection of Monica Tinhofer.*

Bunnies on boat with egg, Anton Reiche #6399, 4-3/4", ca.1910. $200-$300.

Bunny with large eggs in boat, LeCerf #768, ca.1930. *Collection of Rex Morgen.* $150-$200.

Bunny with boat of eggs, Teich #3446, 6-1/4", ca.1920. *Collection of Monica Tinhofer.* $200-$300.

Drawing from an Antique Reiche catalog.

Reverse side.

Bunnies on boat, Anton Reiche #6383,
ca.1910. *Collection of Rex Morgen.* $250.

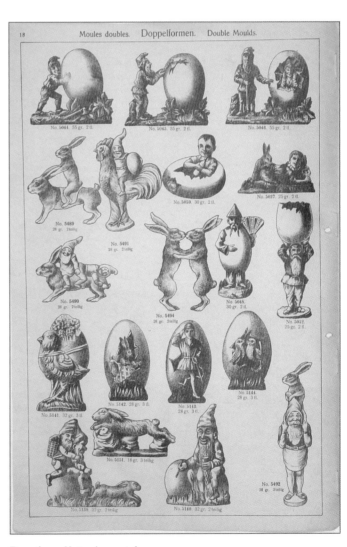

Page from Kutzscher catalog.

Bunny riding bunny, Heris, ca.1930. *Collection and photo courtesy of Erwin and Monika Gschwind.* $400-$500.

Bunny riding fish, Létang #4005, 5", ca.1920. *Collection of Kathryn Campbell.* $450.

Page from catalog showing foil wraps available for molded chocolate.

Chalkware by Kathryn Campbell.

Santa riding bunny, Anton Reiche #21784, 3-1/2", ca.1920. *Collection of Ginny Betourne.* $450.

Postcard style mold of bunny riding dog, Anton Reiche #6697, 5" x 7", ca.1910. $500 and up.

Bunny riding a duck, Heris #3053, 5",
ca.1930. $200-$300.

Bunnies on *see* saw, Laurösch #3087, 7-1/2",
ca.1920. *Collection of Rex Morgen.* $350.

Page from Kutzscher catalog.

Soccer bunny,
Walter #9946, 5",
ca.1940. $250.

Bunny riding rocking horse with
stand, Eppelsheimer #8203, 7",
ca.1930. *Collection of Rex
Morgen.* $300-$450.

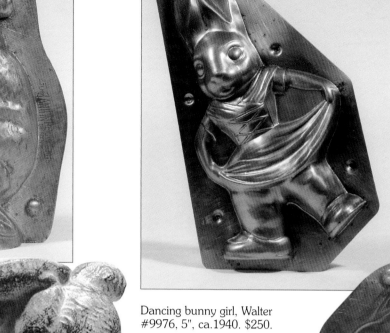

Summersault bunny, Anton Reiche #21878, 4-1/2", ca.1920. *Collection of Moni Marceau.* $250-$400.

Dancing bunny girl, Walter #9976, 5", ca.1940. $250.

Chalkware and photo courtesy of Moni's Folkart.

Soccer playing bunny, Anton Reiche #17766, ca.1920. *Collection of Diane Cazalet.* $250.

Leap frog bunnies, Eppelsheimer #4797, 3-1/2", ca.1930. $175-$250.

Beeswax figures by Kathryn Campbell.

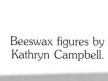

Soccer bunny, #4143, 4",
ca.1930. $150.

Bunny school postcard mold, Anton Reiche #6696,
4-1/2" x 7", ca.1910. $500 and up.

Schoolgirl bunny, Anton
Reiche #30848, 6",
ca.1930. $250-$400.

Bunny getting a spanking, Walter
#8970, 7", ca.1920. $250-$400.

Chalkware
and photo
courtesy of
Vaillancourt
Folk Art.

Nr. 6378. 100 gr. 1 tlg.

Drawing from an Anton Reiche
catalog.

Bunny reading to chicks, Anton Reiche
#6378, 4-1/2", ca.1910. *Collection
and photo Courtesy of Vaillancourt
Folk Art.* $450 and up.

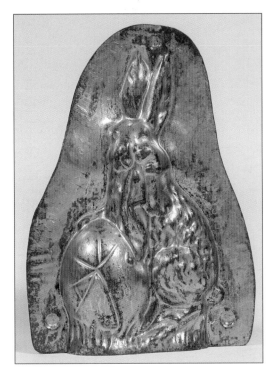

Crying bunny, Kutzscher, 5-1/2", ca.1910.
Collection of Carolyn Deschenes. $250-$350.

Chalkware by Carolyn Deschenes.

Page from Kutzscher catalog.

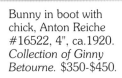

Bunny in boot with
chick, Anton Reiche
#16522, 4", ca.1920.
*Collection of Ginny
Betourne.* $350-$450.

Crying bunny on egg, Kutzscher
#5402, 6", ca.1920. *Collection of
Moni Marceau.* $250-$350.

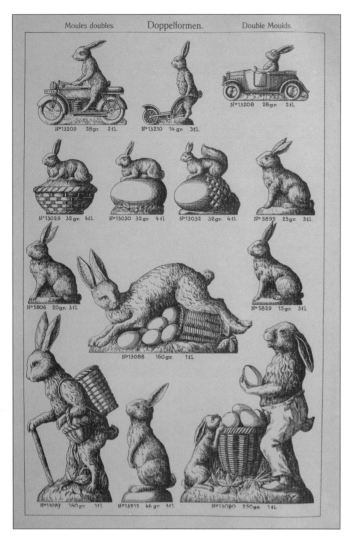

Page from Kutzscher catalog.

Civil War bunny, Anton Reiche #6771, 4-1/2", ca.1910. *Collection of Anne Launius.* $250-$350.

Chalkware by Anne Launius.

Chalkware by Ginny Betourne.

Father Bunny with basket of eggs and baby, Kutzscher #13090, 6-1/2", ca.1930. *Collection of Ginny Betourne.* $450-$650.

54

Traveling bunny with chick, Anton Reiche
#16521, 5", ca.1920. $350-$450.

Page from J.W. Allen catalog.

Bunny with satchel
and pipe, Walter,
5-3/4", ca.1920.
*Collection of
Kathryn Campbell.*
$250.

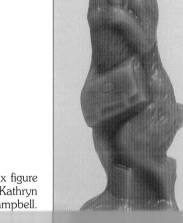

Beeswax figure
by Kathryn
Campbell.

Bunny with cannon, Walter,
6", ca.1920. *Collection of Paul
and Fredricka Schwanka.*
$350 and up.

Marching drummer bunnies, Anton Reiche #6699, 5-1/2" x 4-1/2", ca.1910. *Collection and photo courtesy of Dr. Timberlake.* $500 and up.

Chocolate by Robert Twardzik Confections. Photo by Marcus Pinto.

Vintage postcard.

Bunnies with eggs postcard style mold, Anton Reiche #21333, 5" x 4", ca.1920. *Collection of Carolyn Byrnes.* $500 and up.

Bunny painting egg, Anton Reiche #6414, 4-1/4", ca.1910. $450.

Bunnies painting eggs postcard style mold, Anton Reiche #17829, ca.1920. *Collection of Carolyn Byrnes.* $500 and up.

Chocolate by Robert Twardzik. Photo by Marcus Pinto.

Chocolate by Robert Twardzik Confections. Photo by Marcus Pinto.

Page from Kutzscher catalog.

Postcard mold showing bunnies in a book, Anton
Reiche, 5-1/2" x 3-1/2", ca.1910. *Collection*

Bunny pulling wagon full of eggs postcard mold,
Anton Reiche #10398, 7" x 4", ca.1920.
Collection of Carolyn Byrnes. $500 and up.

Chocolate by Robert Twardzik. Photo by Marcus Pinto.

The exchange of eggs at Easter during the spring-
time is a centuries old custom first celebrated by Chris-
tians. The egg represents rebirth and in many cultures
eggs were colored brightly by boiling them with flowers
and then exchanged with family and friends.

Serenade gone bad, Anton Reiche #17717, 6",
ca.1920. *Collection of Monica Tinhofer.* $150.

Page from Kutzscher catalog.

Two bunnies on egg, Anton
Reiche #5756, 4", ca.1910.
Collection of Rex Morgen. $50.

Chocolate by Morgen
Chocolate.

Bunny driving car egg, Anton Reiche
#5881, ca.1910. $50.

27 I   Osterformen
für Schokolade
(Schaustücke)   Easter Chocolate-Moulds.
Moules à chocolat pour Pâques.
Moldes para chocolate de artículos de Pascua.
Stampi per cioccolato di Pasqua.
Пасхальные формы для шоколада   O 141

Page from Anton Reiche catalog.

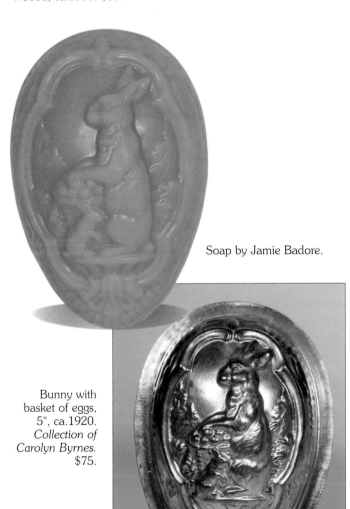

Soap by Jamie Badore.

Bunny with
basket of eggs,
5", ca.1920.
*Collection of
Carolyn Byrnes.*
$75.

Bunnies with big egg, Anton Reiche, ca.1920. *Collection and
photo courtesy of Erwin and Monika Gschwind.* $1,000 and up.

Catalog page showing foil wraps available for molded chocolates.

Egg house front, Teich #1074, 5", ca.1920. *Collection of Carolyn Byrnes.* $250-$450.

Reverse view.

Egg house front, Anton Reiche #26115, 6", ca.1920. *Collection of Moni Marceau.* $750 and up.

Reverse view.

Chalkware and photo courtesy of Moni's Folkart.

Lady bunny with tray of eggs, Anton Reiche #22017, 4-1/2", ca.1920. *Collection of Moni Marceau.* $350.

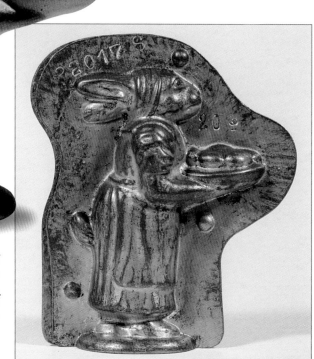

Cast candy mold, #135, 5-1/2", ca.1920. Interior of mold has wonderful detail while the exterior of the mold has none. *Photo courtesy of Kathryn Campbell*. $250.

Bunny with umbrella, Anton Reiche #6339, 5", ca.1910. *Collection of Moni Marceau*. $250-$350.

Chalkware and photo courtesy of Moni Marceau.

Painted beeswax and photo courtesy of Kathryn Campbell.

Chalkware by Penny Burns.

Dressed couple, Anton Reiche #24386, 7", ca.1920. $800.

Art Deco female bunny with basket, 9", ca.1950. *Collection of Carolyn Byrnes.* $250.

Dutch bunny with baskets, Heris #441, 6-1/2", ca.1930. *Collection of Kathryn Campbell.* $250 and up.

Beeswax figure by Kathryn Campbell.

Tux bunny, Obermann, 13-1/2", ca.1930. *Collection of Monica Tinhofer.* $500 and up.

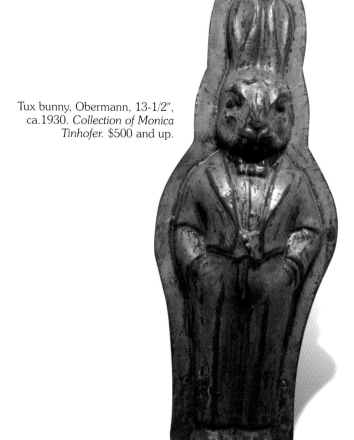

Dutch bunny rides motorcycle, Heris #446, 6-1/2", ca.1930. *Collection of Rex Morgen.* $350.

Drawing from the Heris catalog.

Chalkware by Carolyn Deschenes.

Organ grinder bunny, Walter #8969, 7", ca.1930. *Collection of Carolyn Deschenes.* $350-$450.

Dutch bunny with walking stick, Heris #442, 9-1/2",

Page from a Walter catalog.

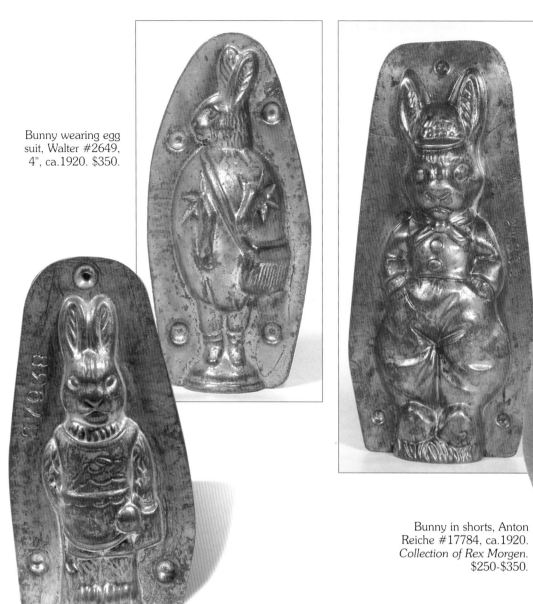

Bunny wearing egg suit, Walter #2649, 4", ca.1920. $350.

Dutch bunny, Anton Reiche #24003, 7", ca.1920. $250-$350.

Bunny in shorts, Anton Reiche #17784, ca.1920. *Collection of Rex Morgen.* $250-$350.

Bunny with shovel and watering can, Anton Reiche #27938, 4", ca.1920. $300-$450.

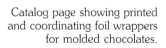

Catalog page showing printed and coordinating foil wrappers for molded chocolates.

Relaxing bunny, Teich, 8", ca.1930.
Collection of Monica Tinhofer. $350.

Bunny with chick
friend, Walter #8227,
5", ca.1920. *Collection
of Ginny Betourne*.
$250-$350.

Overstuffed bunny, Anton
Reiche #28616, 5-1/2",
ca.1930. $200-$250.

Vintage Huyler's Chocolate
postcard.

Sitting Teddy-bear style

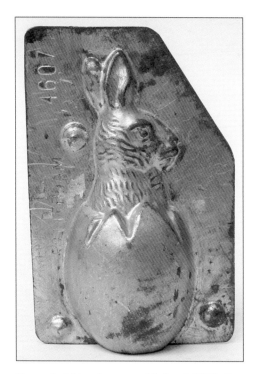

Bunny hatching from egg, Walter #4607, 4",
ca.1920. *Collection of Rex Morgen.* $150.

Bunny with egg holder, Wien #3715, 3-1/2", ca.1930. $150.

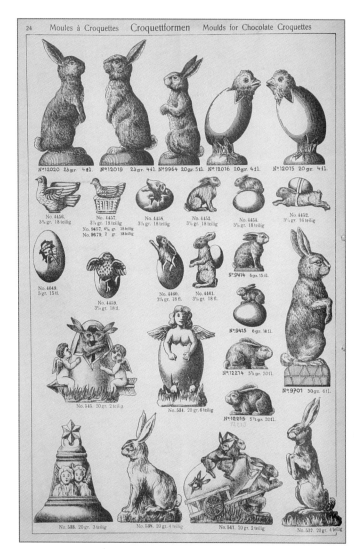

Page from a Kutzscher catalog.

Vintage trade card.

Girl with bunny postcard style mold, Anton Reiche #, 5", ca1920. $650 and up.

Round box, Anton Reiche #6282, 7" diameter, ca.1910. *Collection and photo courtesy of Erwin and Myrtle Gehwind. $1,000 and up.*

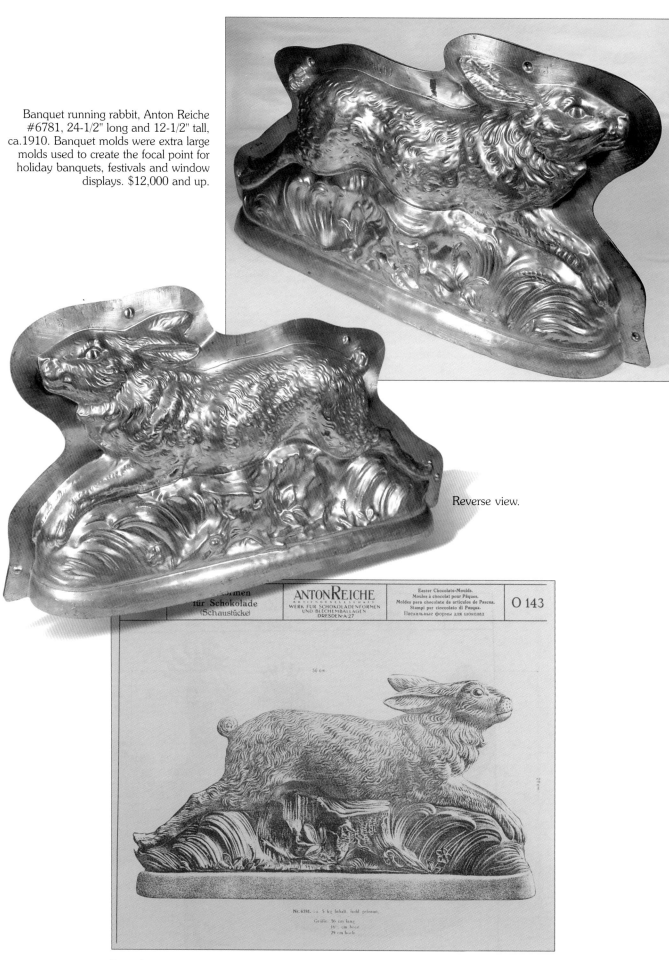

Banquet running rabbit, Anton Reiche #6781, 24-1/2" long and 12-1/2" tall, ca.1910. Banquet molds were extra large molds used to create the focal point for holiday banquets, festivals and window displays. $12,000 and up.

Reverse view.

Page from an Anton Reiche catalog.

Creatures

May bugs or June bugs appear in vast multitudes every year, signaling the onset of summer in Germany. Chocolatiers put out chocolate May bugs with cardboard feet for the children's delight.

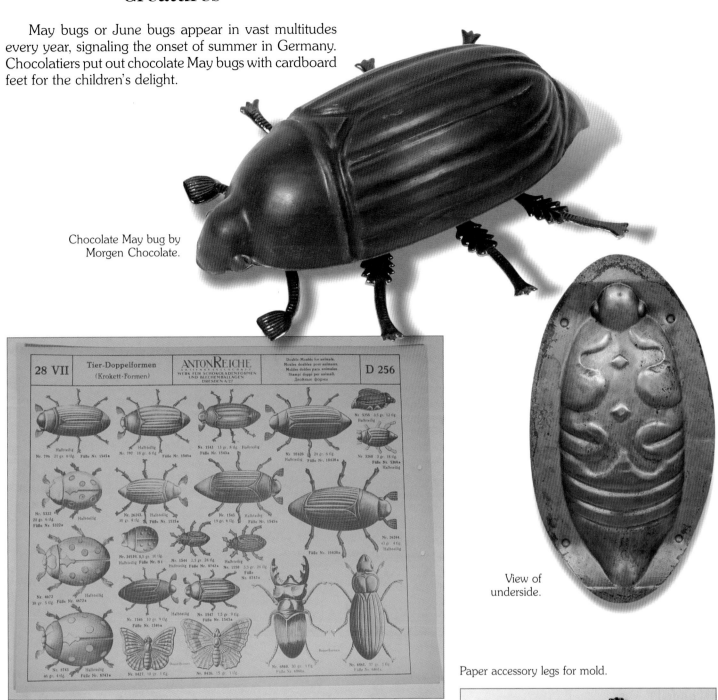

Chocolate May bug by
Morgen Chocolate.

Page from an Anton Reiche catalog.

View of
underside.

Paper accessory legs for mold.

May Bug, #611, 7",

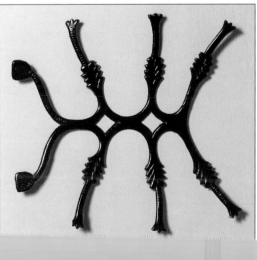

Small May bug, 3", ca.1920. *Collection of my son, Jericho.* $50.

View of underside.

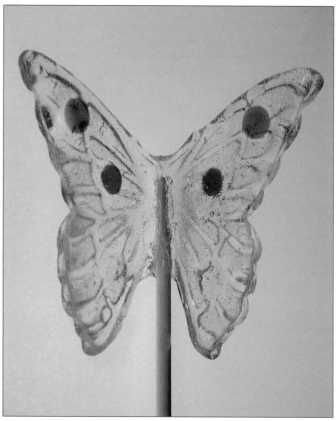

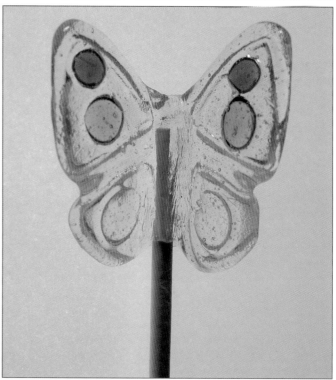

Barley candy by Dorothy Timberlake Candies.

Butterfly flat, Sommet, 4-1/2" x 9", ca.1910.
Collection of Carolyn Byrnes. $150.

Butterfly egg, Hörnlein #7001, 8-1/2", ca.1950. $75.

Ladybug, Walter #2692, 5", ca.1920.
Collection of my son, Richie. $150.

View of the underside.

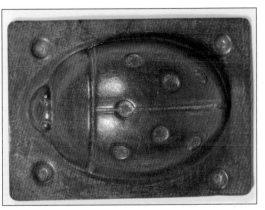

Candy trade card.

View of the underside.

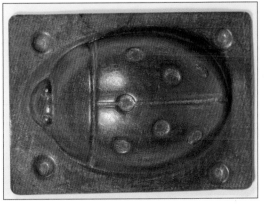

Ladybug, Walter
#2266, 3-1/2", ca.1910.
*Collection of my son,
Jericho.* $125.

Chalkware by Anne Launius
of Holly Ridge Collectibles.

Dressed mole carrying an egg,
#4057, 4-1/2", ca.1940. $150.

"Mr. Frog goes a courting," Anton Reiche #25622, 6",
ca.1920. *Collection of Anne Launius.* $450 and up.

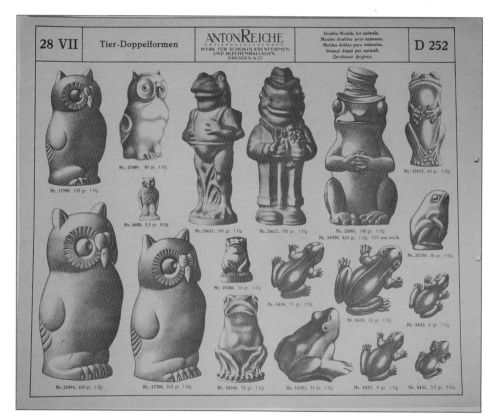

Page from Anton
Reiche catalog.

Frog, Anton Reiche #24166, 4", ca.1920. *Collection of Diane Cazalet.* $200-$350.

Trade card.

Frog, Anton Reiche, 3-3/4", ca.1930. *Collection of Rex Morgen.* $200-$350.

Frog, Anton Reiche #16781, 4", ca.1920. *Collection of Diane Cazalet.* $200-$350.

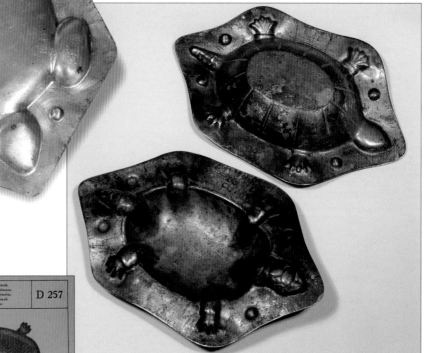

Turtle, Matfer, 8-1/2", ca.1940. *Collection of Carolyn Byrnes.* $250-$350.

Right:
Turtle, 9", ca.1930.
Collection of Diane Cazalet.
$350-$450.

Turtle body.

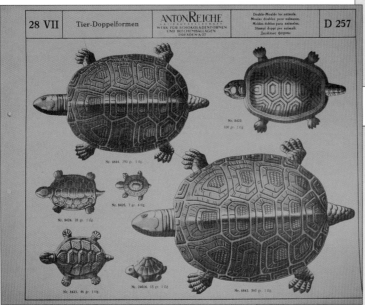

Page from an Anton Reiche catalog.

Turtle shell, Anton Reiche #8422, 5", ca.1920. $350 and up.

Chocolate trade card.

Turtle, Anton Reiche #8423, 3-1/2",
ca.1910. $150.

Soap by Jamie Badore.

Turtle, Anton Reiche
#8424, 3", ca.1910. $150.

Turtle flat, 4" x 10", ca.1920. *Collection of Carolyn Byrnes.* $150.

Right:
Stand up candy counter card.

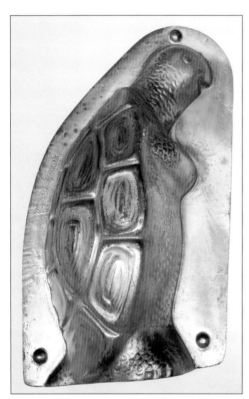

Turtle, Anton Reiche #28807, 6-1/2",
ca.1930. $150-$250.

Goat, Walter #4600,
2-1/4", ca.1920.
$250.

Chocolate trade card.

Chalkware by Anne Launius.

Goat, Anton Reiche #8540,
4-1/2", ca.1910. $450.

Large goat, Anton Reiche #8539,
5-1/2", ca.1910. $650.

JACOB STUVÉ

NOUGAT- EN DESSERTWERK.-FABRIEK

Telefoon 2707 — BREDA

WETTIG GEDEPONEERD

Page from original
Anton Reiche
catalog.

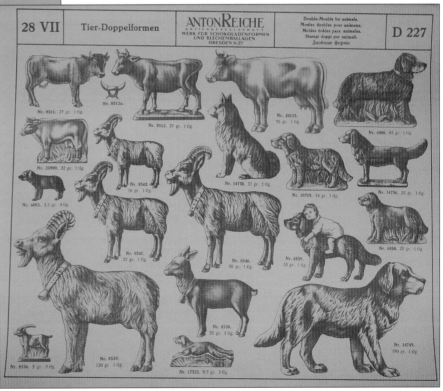

Large chicken in basket, Anton Reiche #6724, 17", ca.1910.
Collection of Monica Tinhofer. $5,000 and up.

Hinged rooster, Van Emden Co. NY, Made in Germany, #8757, 4", ca.1930. $150.

Page from original Anton Reiche catalog.
Collection of Monica Tinhofer.

Vintage postcard.

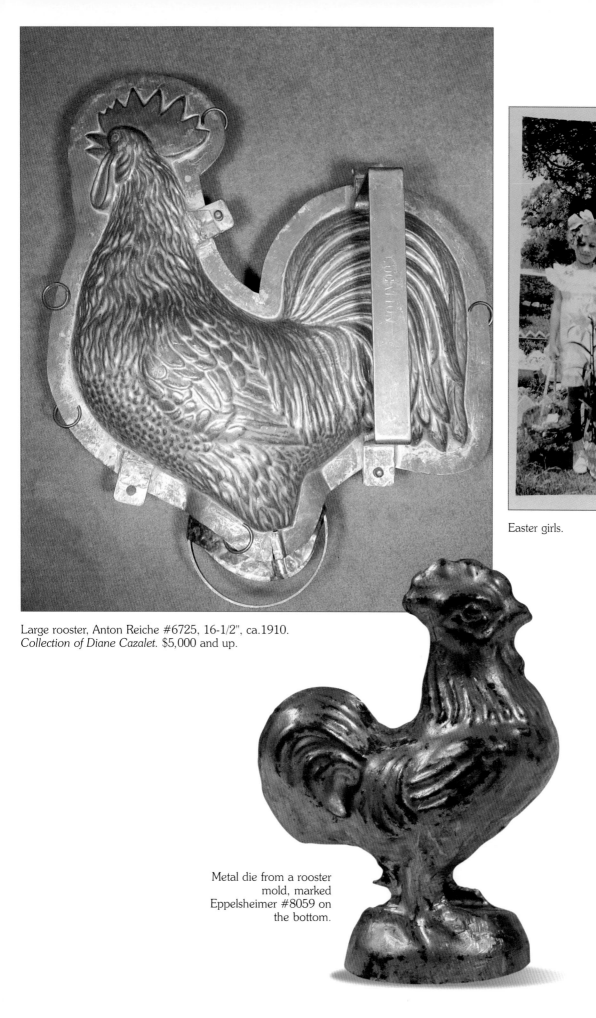

Large rooster, Anton Reiche #6725, 16-1/2", ca.1910.
Collection of Diane Cazalet. $5,000 and up.

Easter girls.

Metal die from a rooster
mold, marked
Eppelsheimer #8059 on
the bottom.

79

Chalkware by Anne Launius.

Rooster preacher, Anton Reiche #27879, 4-1/2", ca.1920. $250-$350.

Preacher's wife, Anton Reiche #27880, 4", ca.1920. *Collection of Rex Morgen.* $250-$350.

Serious rooster, Anton Reiche #29301, 6", ca.1920. *Collection of Carolyn Byrnes.* $300-$400.

Rooster man and egg, 3-1/2", ca.1930. $350 and up.

Dressed mother hen, #320, 3-3/4", ca.1920. *Collection of Kathryn Campbell.* $250.

Chalkware by Kathryn Campbell of Bittersweethouse.com.

Huyler's postcard.

Beeswax figures by Kathryn Campbell.

Hen house, Anton Reiche #6821, 4", ca.1910.
Collection of Anne Launius. $350 and up.

Chalkware by Anne Launius.

Back of hen house.

Reverse.

Boy riding chick, Anton Reiche #6531,
4", ca.1910. $350-$450.

Chocolate by Morgen Chocolate.

Chalkware by Carolyn Deschenes.

Hatching rooster, Walter #4606,
3-1/2", ca.1930. $150.

Chick, Anton Reiche #33254, 2-1/2", ca.1940. $125.

"Angry Chick," papier mâché by Ginny Betourne. Inspired by antique chocolate molds.

Easter postcard.

Bunny pulling chick in egg car, Walter #8428, 4-1/2", ca.1930. $175-$250.

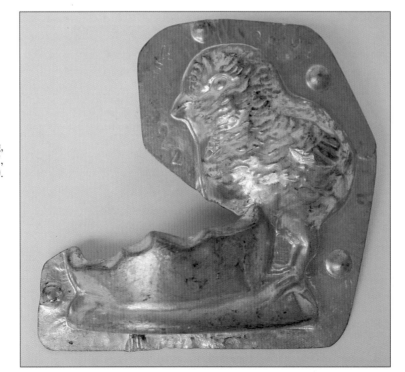

Chick with open egg, Teich #3610, 4-1/4", ca.1930. $150.

Tiny chicken, #14000, 2", ca.1920. Produced
by the Swiss mold manufacturer Merker. $150.

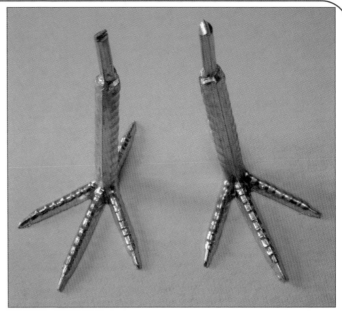

Metal legs for chicken.

This view of the mold shows where
accessory legs would be added.

Close-up of the running Mercury
trademark representing Merker.

Rooster, Laurösch #365, 10", ca.1950. *Chocolate
and mold photo courtesy of Calico Chocolates.* $250.

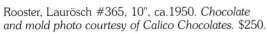

Chick pulling cart with hatching chick,
#288, 6-1/4", ca.1930. $175-$250.

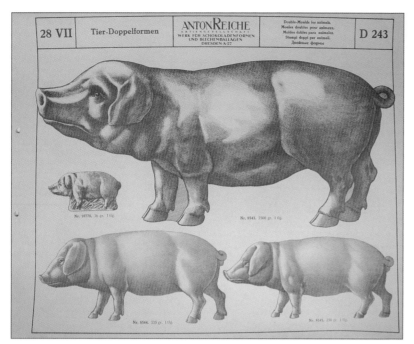

Nr. 10776. 36 gr. 1 tlg.   Nr. 8543. 2500 gr. 1 tlg.

Nr. 8544. 335 gr. 1 tlg.   Nr. 8545. 250 gr. 1 tlg.

Page from original Anton
Reiche catalog.

Lost lamb, 2-1/2", ca.1930. $150.

Right:
Pig pulling cart to
market, Walter, 6",
ca.1930. $250-$350.

Large pig, Anton Reiche #8543, 15" ca.1920.
Collection of Diane Cazalet. $3,000 and up.

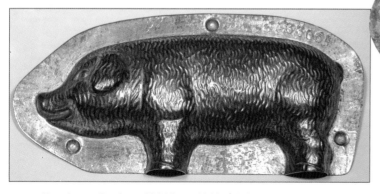

Pig with bag on back, Walter, 3-3/4", ca.1930.
Collection of Monica Tinhofer. $250.

Pig, Anton Reiche #33064, ca.1940. $150.

Page showing foil wrap designs for molded chocolate.

Laying lamb, Anton Reiche #28618, 4", ca.1930. *Collection of Rex Morgen.* $150-$200.

Chocolate by Morgen Chocolate.

Lamb, Anton Reiche #5293, 5", ca.1920. *Collection of Kathryn Campbell.* $250.

Chalkware by Kathryn Campbell.

Lamb, 6", ca.1940. *Collection of Carolyn Byrnes.* $250.

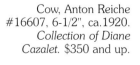

Soap by Jamie Badore.

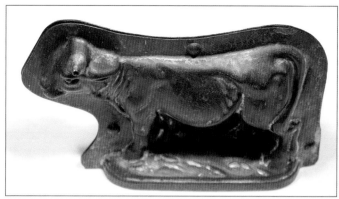

Cow, Anton Reiche #8506, 7-1/2", ca.1910. *Collection of Diane Cazalet.* $350 and up.

Laying cow, Anton Reiche #25506, 7", ca.1920. *Collection of Diane Cazalet.* $350 and up.

Calf, #3714, 6", ca.1940. $250.

Cow, Anton Reiche #16607, 6-1/2", ca.1920. *Collection of Diane Cazalet.* $350 and up.

Cow, Anton Reiche #24123, 5", ca.1920.
Collection of Rex Morgen. $250 and up.

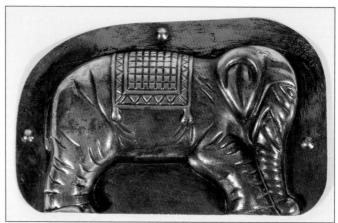

Elephant with blanket, Vormenfabriek
#16160, 6-1/4", ca.1960. $150.

Stollwerck's Chocolate Card.

Dog sitting, Anton Reiche #14758, 4-1/2",
ca.1920. *Collection of Diane Cazalet.* $175-$250.

"*Reflections,*" Anton Reiche #8598, 5-1/2", ca.1910.
Collection and chalkware by Ginny Betourne. $150-$250.

Sitting Elephant,
Sommet, 10" ca.1920.
$350-$450.

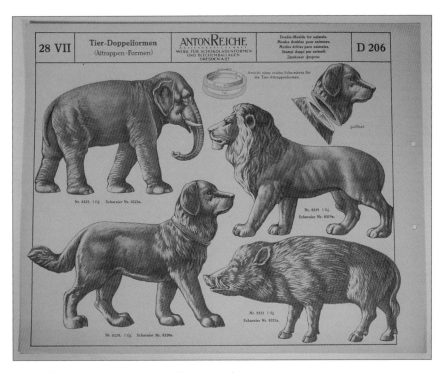

Page from original Anton Reiche catalog.

Poodle in newspaper hat, Anton Reiche #6887, 3-1/4",
ca.1910. *Collection of Diane Cazalet.* $250.

Four piece dog, Anton
Reiche #8320, 7-1/2",
ca.1910. *Collection of
Carolyn Byrnes.* $650
and up.

Bulldog, Anton Reiche #25455,
5-1/2", ca.1920. $250.

Close-up of head.

Dachshund, Walter, 6-1/2" ca.1920. *Collection of Diane Cazalet.* $375.

Dachshund, Laurösch #606, 7", ca.1920. $350.

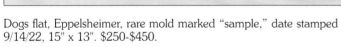

Dogs flat, Eppelsheimer, rare mold marked "sample," date stamped 9/14/22, 15" x 13". $250-$450.

Dachshund, Laurösch #4115, 4-1/2", ca.1920. *Collection of Diane Cazalet.* $350.

Detail of one section.

Marking detail.

Scottie dog, Anton Reiche #32847, 5", ca.1930. *Collection of Anne Launius.* $250-$350.

Scottie dog, Anton Reiche #32785, 9", ca.1930. $350 and up.

Chalkware by Anne Launius.

Additional view.

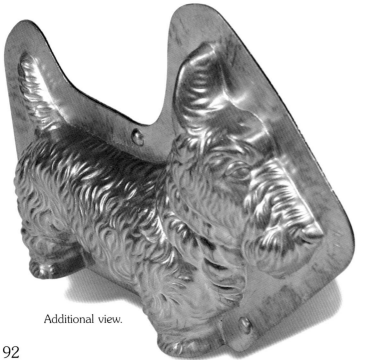

Additional view.

Art Deco Scottie dog, Anton Reiche #28843, 4-1/2",
ca.1930. *Collection of Moni Marceau.* $250.

Page from original 1933 Stollwerck's catalog.

Two fan flats of dog and cat faces, Létang, Cats #1607, Dogs
#1608, ca.1920. *Collection of Rex Morgen.* $250.

Pair of dogs, Eppelsheimer, 4-1/2", ca.1930. $150.

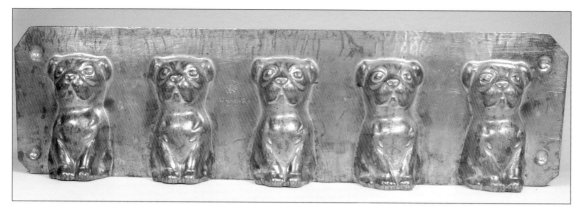

Dogs, Eppelsheimer #7464, 11", ca.1930. $250.

Pair of cats, Eppelsheimer, 4-3/4", ca.1930. $150.

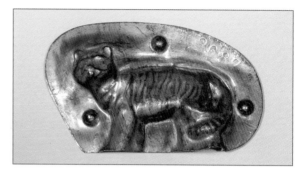

Cat, Anton Reiche #8687, 3-1/2", ca.1920. *Collection of Diane Cazalet.* $200-$300.

Page from original Anton Reiche catalog.

Candy trade card.

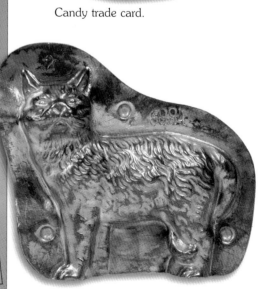

Standing cat, Anton Reiche #6884, 4-1/2", ca.1910. $250-$350.

Sitting Persian, Eppelsheimer #8230, 10", ca.1920. $500 and up.

Cat, #3687, 4-1/2", ca.1920. *Collection of Kathryn Campbell.* $250-$350.

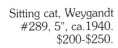

Beeswax by Kathryn Campbell.

Cat, Anton Reiche #32843, 7-1/2", ca.1940. $350-$450.

Sitting cat, Weygandt #289, 5", ca.1940. $200-$250.

Sitting cat, Anton Reiche #8659, 3", ca.1910. $250.

Candy trade card.

Page from original Anton Reiche catalog.

Crying cat, #5408, 4", ca.1910. *Collection of Ginny Betourne.* $250-$350.

Chimpanzee, Anton Reiche #14773, 3-1/2", ca.1920. $250.

Chimp riding fish, Anton Reiche #8731, 5", ca.1910. *Collection of Diane Cazalet.* $350 and up.

96

Chocolate by Morgen Chocolate.

Teddy Bear body, Walter, 5-3/4", ca.1920. *Collection of Paul and Fredricka Schwanka.* $450 and up.

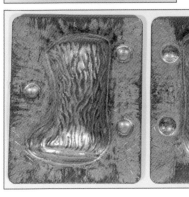

Legs for Teddy Bear, Walter, 2-3/4", ca.1920. *Collection of Paul and Fredricka Schwanka.*

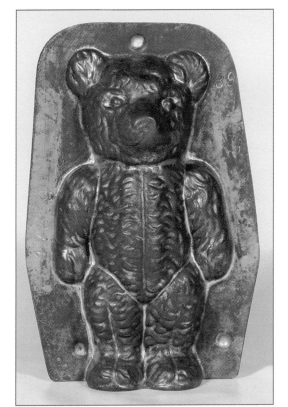

Teddy Bear, Anton Reiche #17569, 5", ca.1920. $350-$500.

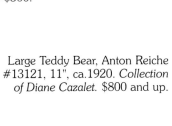

Large Teddy Bear, Anton Reiche #13121, 11", ca.1920. *Collection of Diane Cazalet.* $800 and up.

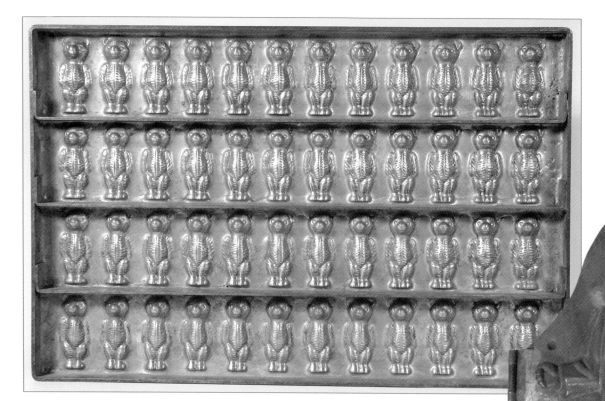

Teddy Bear flat, 11" x 13", ca.1930. $350.

Teddy Bear, Vormenfabriek #16159, 5", ca.1950. $150-$200.

Sitting Teddy Bear, Anton Reiche #25940, 3-3/4", ca.1920. *Collection of Diane Cazalet.* $250-$350.

Russian bear trainer, Anton Reiche #10781, 8 1/8", ca.1910. *Collection and photo courtesy of William Timberlake M.D.* $800 and up.

Beeswax by BitterSweetHouse.com.

Hinged sitting Teddy Bear, Anton Reiche #17518, 2-1/2", ca.1920. *Collection of Diane Cazalet.* $250-$350.

Page from original Anton Reiche catalog.
Collection of Monica Tinhofer.

Walking bear, Anton Reiche #16758,
7", ca.1920. $250-$300.

Sitting bear, Anton Reiche
#7943, 3", ca.1910. $250.

Trained bear, Anton Reiche #10780, 9-1/8", ca.1910. *Collection
and photo courtesy of William Timberlake M.D.* $800 and up.

Five piece bear, Anton Reiche
#8328, body 6", head 2-1/2",
ca.1910. *Collection and photo
courtesy of William Timberlake
M.D.* $650 and up.

Standing bear, Anton Reiche #17487, 4-1/2", ca.1920. *Collection of Diane Cazalet.* $350.

Rocker base chimpanzee, Anton Reiche #25741, 4-1/2", ca.1930. *Collection of Diane Cazalet.* $350.

Polar Bear drinking from bottle, 8", ca.1930. $250.

Rocker base Teddy Bear, Anton Reiche #25739, 4-1/2", ca.1930. *Collection of Diane Cazalet.* $350.

Rocker base elephant, Anton Reiche #25780, 4-1/2", ca.1930. *Collection of Diane Cazalet.* $350.

Rocker base bunny, Anton Reiche #25738, 4-1/2", ca.1930. *Collection of Diane Cazalet.* $350.

Large deer, Sommet, 11-1/2", ca.1910.
Collection of Anne Launius. $800 and up.

Chalkware by Anne Launius of
Holly Ridge Collectibles.

Face detail.

Rocker base Santa, Anton Reiche #25737, 4-1/2", ca.1930.
Collection of Diane Cazalet. $350 and up.

Rocker base Indian, Anton Reiche #25740, 4-1/2",
ca.1930. *Collection of Diane Cazalet.* $350.

Squirrel with nut, Anton Reiche #8691, 5", ca.1930.
Collection of Moni Marceau. $250-$350.

Squirrel on branch, Sommet, 10-1/2", ca.1920.
Collection of Diane Cazalet. $800 and up.

THANKSGIVING GREETINGS

Thanksgiving postcard.

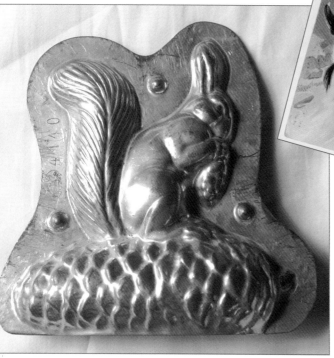

Squirrel on pinecone, Laurösch #4140, 6",
ca.1920. *Collection of Monica Tinhofer.* $250-$350.

GE BROS. CO., CHICAGO, U. S. A.

CHOCOLATE METAL MOULDS

SPECIAL CIRCULAR ON REQUEST

Page from an original
Savage Bros. catalog.

Giant turkey, Anton Reiche #20904, 19",
ca.1920. *Collection and photo courtesy of
William Timberlake M.D.* $5,000 and up.

Detail of pieces.

Three piece turkey, Anton Reiche #14077,
4-1/2", ca.1920. $450-$600.

Three piece turkey,
Eppelsheimer #4923,
9", ca.1920. *Collection
of Diane Cazalet.*
$450-$600

103

Tin Chocolate Moulds

Moulded chocolate is a very desirable item for the confectioner because it is especially profitable, due to freedom from loss and spoilage. It is easy to make and offers good value to your customers.

The moulds are filled with chocolate and put aside to cool. As the temperature drops, the chocolate loosens from the mould and may be easily removed when cool.

To cast hollow pieces, simply fill the mould with chocolate at dipping consistency and shake out the excess chocolate immediately. All the numbers listed on the following pages are ready for immediate delivery.

We carry in stock, among other food products, a full line of chocolate suitable for bar, mould and coating purposes.

Turkey Designs for Thanksgiving

No. 5041. Three part mould. 4½ ozs. 3½ in. high. Each $2.50

No. 4920. Two part mould. 6½ ozs. 4¾ in. high. Each $2.50

No. 6514. Two part mould. 3⅝ ozs. 3⅜ in. high. Each $1.50

No. 644. Two part mould. 16 ozs. 7½ in. high. Each $6.00

Page from original J.W. Allen catalog.

Menagerie, Collection of the Dorchy Family,

Walking tiger, Anton Reiche #8326, 8", ca.1910. *Collection of Diane Cazalet.* $250-$350.

Owl, 4", ca.1930. *Collection of Rex Morgen.* $250.

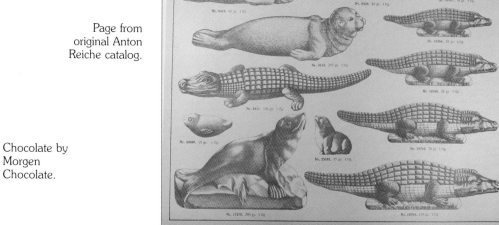

Alligator, Létang #3719, 11", ca.1920. *Collection of Diane Cazalet.* $450 and up.

Page from original Anton Reiche catalog.

Chocolate by Morgen Chocolate.

104

Alligator, 7", ca.1930.
Collection of Monica Tinhofer. $250.

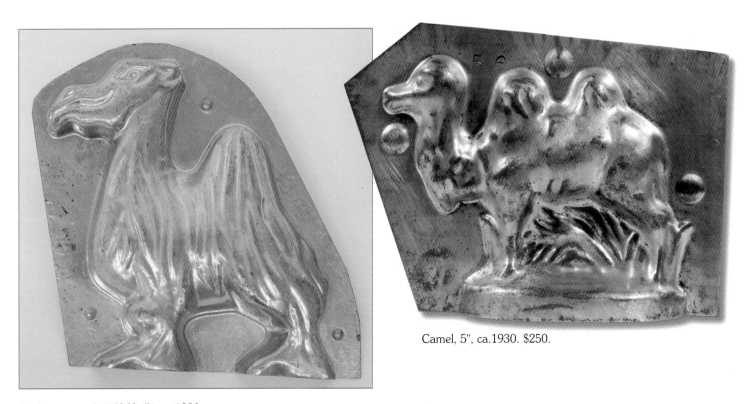

Art Deco camel, #4960, 5", ca.1930.
Collection of Rex Morgen. $250-$350.

Camel, 5", ca.1930. $250.

Camel, Anton Reiche #8387, 6", ca.1910.
Collection of Diane Cazalet. $350.

Page from original Anton Reiche catalog.

105

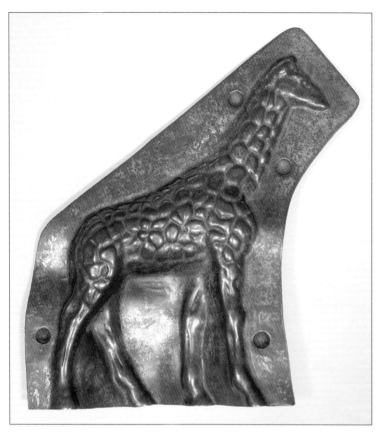

Giraffe, Létang #3710, 5-1/4", ca.1920.
Collection of Diane Cazalet. $350.

Giraffe, Sommet #2029, 6", ca.1920. $250.

Zebra, Kutzscher #5667, 5",
ca.1920. $250-$400.

Page from original
Kutzscher catalog.

Kangaroo, Kutzscher #5885, 5-1/2",
ca.1920. $250-$400.

106

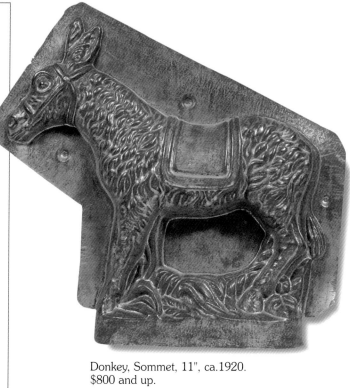

Donkey, Sommet, 11", ca.1920.
$800 and up.

Kangaroo, Anton Reiche #17590, 6",
ca.1920. *Collection of Erwin and
Monika Gschwind.* $450.

Donkey, Anton Reiche
#6614, 6", ca.1910.
$450 and up.

Buffalo, LeCerf #1757, 6",
ca.1940. *Collection of Robert
Byrnes.* $350-$550.

Chocolate by Morgen
Chocolate.

107

Donkey, Anton Reiche #29575, 4", ca.1920. $200.

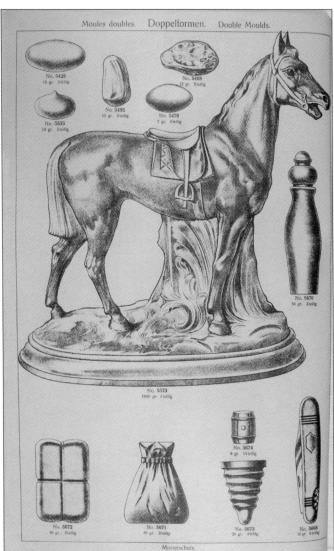

Page from original Kutzscher catalog.

Chocolat Guerin-
Boutron trade card.

Horse with saddle, Kutzscher #5581, 3-5/8",
ca.1920. *Collection of Carolyn Byrnes*. $250.

Many artists are now enjoying these wonderful old cast molds for use with beeswax, chocolate, chalkware, and of course hard candy. The detail achieved is exquisite but can present more of a challenge to work with compared to tin chocolate molds.

Interior detail.

Beeswax figure and photo by Kathryn Campbell.

Exterior detail of three-piece horse mold, marked aK #245, 9".
Photo courtesy of Kathryn Campbell. $250.

Horse, Anton Reiche #25061, 5", ca.1920.
Collection of Rex Morgen. $175-$250.

Swimming ducks, Anton Reiche #28623, 6", ca.1930. $175-$250.

Art Deco style horse, Létang #4275, 4", ca.1930. *Collection of Rex Morgen.* $250-$350.

Chocolate by Morgen Chocolate.

Catalog page showing foil wraps available for molded chocolate.

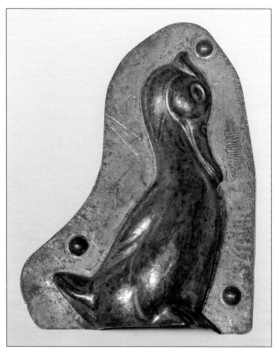

Duck, Anton Reiche #25383, 4-1/2", ca.1920.
Collection Diane Cazalet. $150.

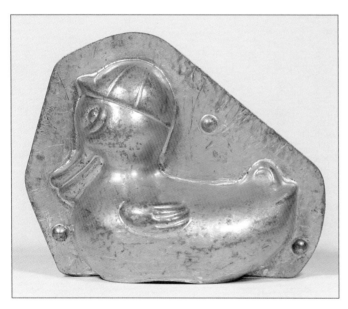

Duck wearing cap, Anton Reiche
#23011, 5-3/4", ca.1930. *Collection
of Rex Morgen.* $150.

Duck, 6", ca.1920. $250.

Swan, Walter #8487, 5", ca.1920.
$250-$350.

Page from original Laurösch catalog.

Peacock, Sommet, 10-1/2",
ca.1920. *Collection of Diane
Cazalet.* $800 and up.

Sparrow, Anton Reiche #14736, 5", ca.1920.
$350-$450.

Detail of underside.

Stork with babies,
Létang #4213, 9",
ca.1920. *Collection
and photo courtesy
of William
Timberlake
M.D.* $800
and up.

111

Papier mâché penguin hatching, inspired by antique chocolate molds, created by Susan Brack.

Penguin, Walter, 4", ca.1930. *Collection of Diane Cazalet.* $200-$250.

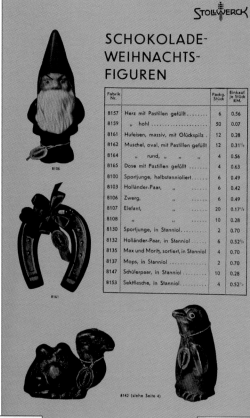

STOLLWERCK

SCHOKOLADE-WEIHNACHTS-FIGUREN

Fabrik Nr.		Packg. Stück	Einkauf je Stück RM.
8157	Herz mit Pastillen gefüllt........	6	0.56
8159	„ hohl	50	0.07
8161	Hufeisen, massiv, mit Glückspilz .	12	0.28
8162	Muschel, oval, mit Pastillen gefüllt	12	0.31½
8164	„ rund, „ „ „	4	0.56
8165	Dose mit Pastillen gefüllt	4	0.63
8100	Sportjunge, halbstanniolert.......	6	0.49
8103	Holländer-Paar,.......	6	0.42
8106	Zwerg, „	6	0.49
8107	Elefant, „	20	0.17½
8108	„ „	10	0.28
8130	Sportjunge, in Stanniol.........	2	0.70
8132	Holländer-Paar, in Stanniol.....	6	0.52½
8135	Max und Moritz, sortiert, in Stanniol	4	0.70
8137	Mops, in Stanniol	2	0.70
8147	Schülerpaar, in Stanniol........	10	0.28
8153	Sektflasche, in Stanniol..........	4	0.52½

8106

8161

8142 (siehe Seite 4)

Page from original 1933 Stollwerck's catalog.

Penguin, Anton Reiche #25790, 3", ca.1920. $150-$250.

Dressed penguin, #13079, 6", ca.1920. *Collection of Diane Cazalet.* $350-$450.

112

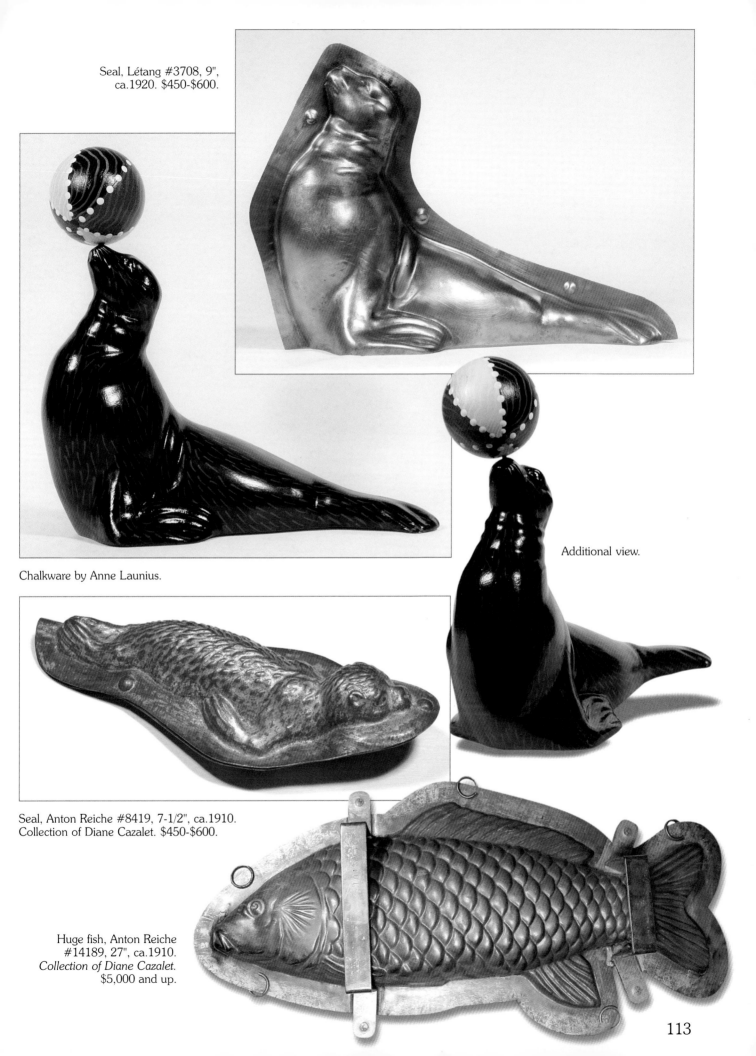

Seal, Létang #3708, 9",
ca.1920. $450-$600.

Chalkware by Anne Launius.

Additional view.

Seal, Anton Reiche #8419, 7-1/2", ca.1910.
Collection of Diane Cazalet. $450-$600.

Huge fish, Anton Reiche
#14189, 27", ca.1910.
Collection of Diane Cazalet.
$5,000 and up.

113

Flounder, ca.1900. *Collection of Rex Morgen.* $250.

Soap by Jamie Badore.

Fish with an open top, Anton Reiche #28685, 7-3/4", ca.1920. *Collection of Carolyn Byrnes.* $175.

Stylized dolphin, *Collection of The Dorchy Family.* $650.

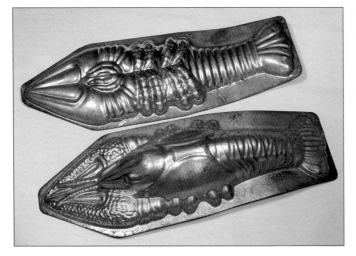

Lobster, Létang #857, 12", ca.1900. *Collection of Diane Cazalet.* $250-$400.

114

Grasshopper, Létang #2694, 8", ca.1910.
Collection of Diane Cazalet. $800 and up.

Page from original Létang catalog.

Page from original Létang catalog.

Siren, GPL #722, 7", ca.1900, tin washed copper. *Collection of Diane Cazalet.* $750-$850.

Série D

MOULES EN ÉTAIN POUR PIÈCES MONTÉES

LETANG FILS, 108, RUE VIEILLE-DU-TEMPLE, PARIS

Page from original Létang catalog.

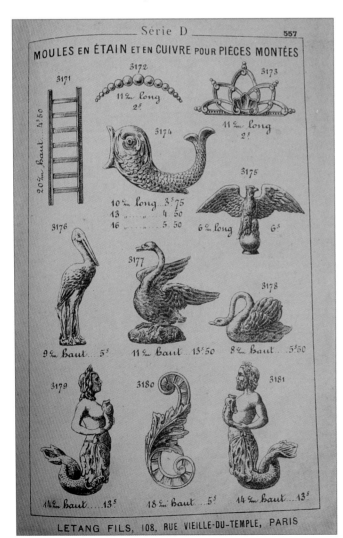

Série D   557

MOULES EN ÉTAIN ET EN CUIVRE POUR PIÈCES MONTÉES

LETANG FILS, 108, RUE VIEILLE-DU-TEMPLE, PARIS

Griffin, Létang #2496, 6", ca.1900. $800-$850.

Page from original
Létang catalog.

Page from original Létang catalog.

Dragon, Létang #2264, 8-1/2",
ca.1900. $800-$850.

Chalkware by Anne Launius.

Chalkware front.

117

Characters

Page from original Anton Reiche catalog.

Pilgrim Boy with turkey and rifle,
Eppelsheimer #8227, 8-3/4", ca.1930.
Collection of Vaillancourt. $450 and up.

Chalkware and photo
courtesy of Vaillancourt
Folk Art.

Alice in Wonderland,
Anton Reiche #23720, 5",
ca.1920. $250.

Advertisement for Peter's Chocolates.

Mad Hatter, Anton Reiche #23719,
5", ca.1920. $250.

118

Brothers, Anton Reiche #7555, 5-1/2",
ca.1920. $250-$300.

Musician in chocolate by Morgen Chocolate.

Reverse view.

Musician mold, Anton Reiche #24924, 3-1/2",
ca.1920. *Collection of Rex Morgen.* $150.

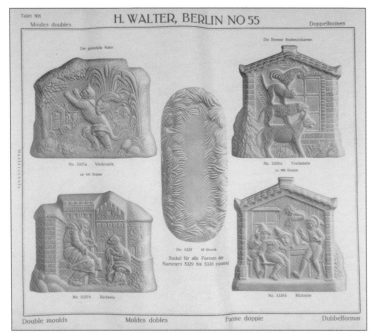

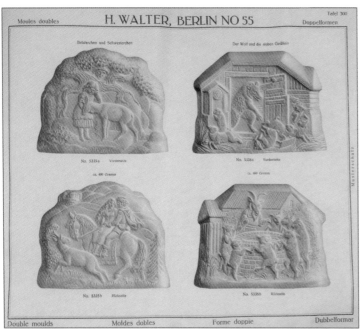

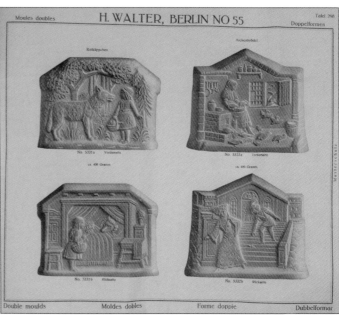

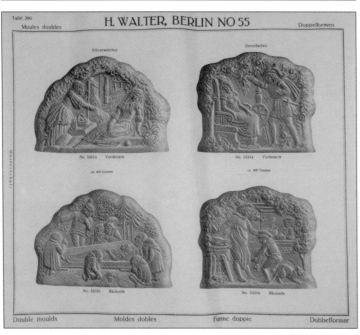

Pages from Walter catalog showing fairytale molds.

Reverse.

Puss n' boots scene, Walter, made in Germany, 6-1/2", ca.1920. *Collection of Paul and Fredricka Schwanka.* $500 and up.

Cinderella scene, Walters 6-1/4" ca1920. *Collection of Paul and Fredricka Schwanka.* $500 and up.

Egg with Cinderella Scene, 6", ca.1920. $150.

Reverse.

Male rider for motorcycle, Walter #8439, 4-3/4", ca.1930. $250.

Motorcycle, Walter #8438, 6", ca.1930. $250.

Female rider for motorcycle, Walter #8440, 4-1/2", ca.1930. $250.

Chocolate by Morgen Chocolate.

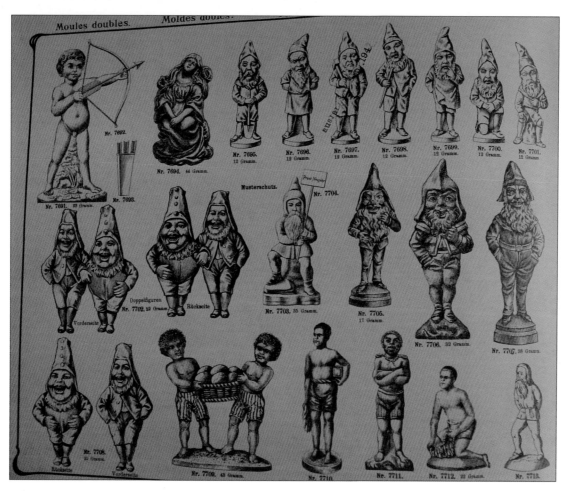

Page from original Anton Reiche catalog. *Collection of Monica Tinhofer.*

Cacao harvesters, Anton Reiche
#7709, 3-1/2", ca.1920. $250-$300.

Reverse.

Chalkware and photo
courtesy Moni's Folkart.

Ice skating girl, Anton Reiche #26218, 5", ca.1920.
Collection of Moni Marceau. $250-$350.

Boy throwing
snowballs, Anton
Reiche #26220, 5",
ca.1920. *Collection
of Moni Marceau.*
$250-$350.

Max and Moritz were characters from German fairytales. They were two naughty little boys who were always getting into mischief based on the stories by *Wilhelm Busch*.

Bust of Max and Moritz, 4", ca.1920.
Collection of Diane Cazalet. $200-$250.

Max and Moritz, Anton Reiche #7539, 4", ca.1920.
Collection of Carolyn Byrnes. $250.

Max and Moritz, 6",
ca.1930. *Collection of Diane
Cazalet.* $200-$250.

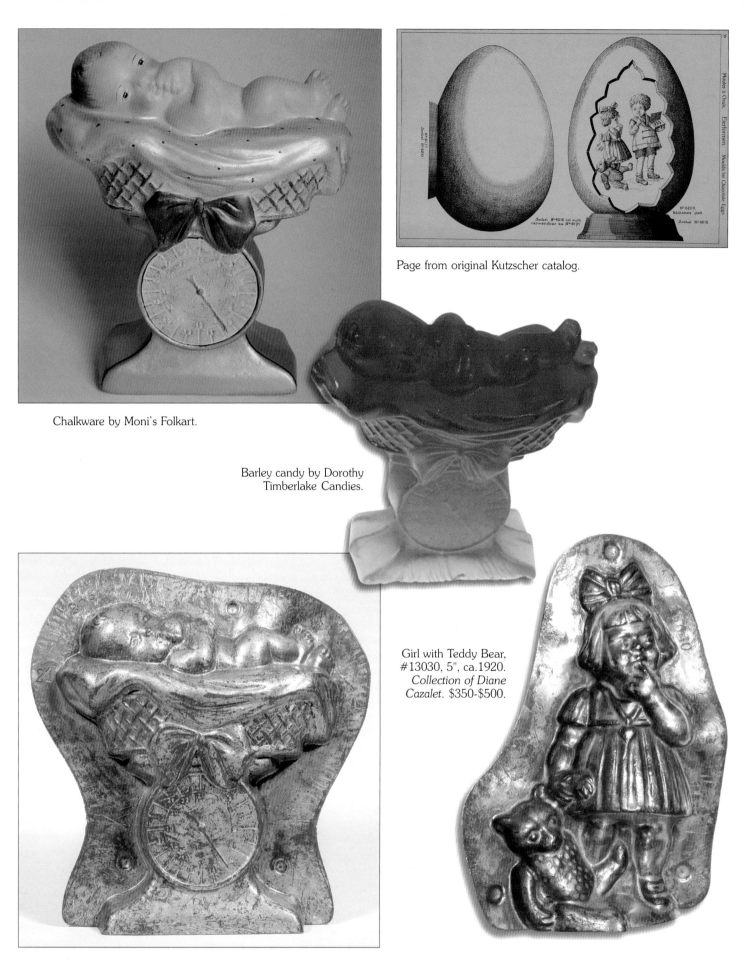

Page from original Kutzscher catalog.

Chalkware by Moni's Folkart.

Barley candy by Dorothy Timberlake Candies.

Girl with Teddy Bear, #13030, 5", ca.1920. *Collection of Diane Cazalet.* $350-$500.

Baby on scale, Anton Reiche #29846, 7", ca.1930. *Collection of Moni Marceau.* $800 and up.

Little Jane with watering can, Anton Reiche #24222, 3", ca.1920. $150-$200.

Boy eating candy, #13059, 5-1/2", ca.1920. $275-$350.

Photo of German schoolboy with cone of candy, ca.1920.

Ghirardelli coloring book ca.1900.

Sailor, Anton Reiche #26899, 5-1/2", ca.1920. *Collection of Diane Cazalet.* $200.

127

Popeye, Walters #9034, 7",
ca.1940. $800.

Indian, 4", ca.1930. *Collection
of Carolyn Byrnes.* $50.

Chocolate by Morgen
Chocolate.

Sailor, Anton Reiche
#23133, 5-1/2", ca.1920.
*Collection of Monica
Tinhofer.* $200.

Indian man, Vormenfabriek, 4", ca.1950.
Collection of Carolyn Byrnes. $50.

Indian woman, Vormenfabriek, 4", ca.1950.
Collection of Carolyn Byrnes. $50.

Indian riding horse, Anton Reiche #27113,
3", ca. 1930. $175-$250.

Indian paperweight with
feather letter opener, marked
Ben Mohr Chocolate Moulds.

Art Deco Indian, Anton Reiche
#13344, 5-3/4", ca.1930. *Collection of
Rex Morgen.* $250-$300.

Man with pigs, Anton Reiche #31311,
7-1/2", ca.1930. *Collection of Anne
Launius.* $350-$450.

Chalkware by Anne Launius.

Chimney sweep, 6", ca.1930.
Collection of Monica Tinhofer. $250.

Man riding pig, Teich #3105, 6-3/4",
ca.1930. *Collection of Monica Tinhofer.*
$300-$400.

Chimney sweep, Walter #1711, 5",
ca.1920. $150-$200.

Chimney sweep, Anton
Reiche #27132, 6-3/4",
ca.1920. $250.

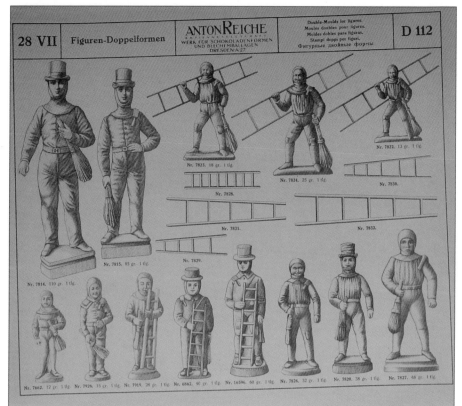

Page from original Anton Reiche catalog.

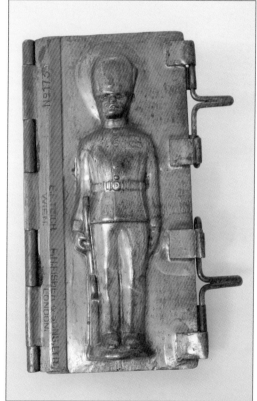

Soldier, Teich #1733, 6", ca.1930.
Collection of Rex Morgen. $200-$250.

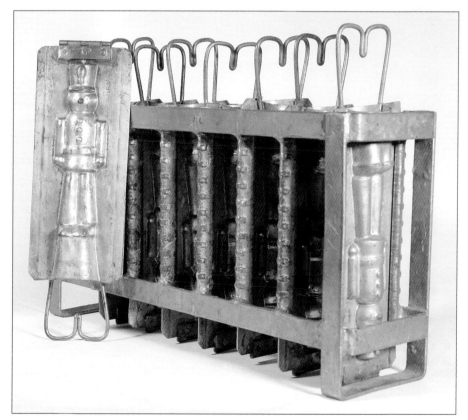

Rack of eight soldiers, Eppelsheimer #8296, 8", marked June 1940. $500.

Chocolate soldiers by Morgen Chocolate.

Soldier, Létang #4352, 4 1/8", ca.1930.
Collection of Rex Morgen. $200.

Soldier, Létang #4350, 4", ca.1930.
Collection of Rex Morgen. $200.

Soldier, Létang #4351, 4", ca.1930.
Collection of Rex Morgen. $200.

Chalkware and photo courtesy of Moni Marceau.

Angel, banquet ice cream mold, #582, DRGM, 11". $800 and up.

Child with cookie, Anton Reiche #24113, 5", ca.1920. *Collection of Moni Marceau.* $250-$350.

Child with hands in muff, Anton Reiche #24114, 5", ca.1920. *Collection of Moni Marceau.* $250-$350.

Inside.

Chocolate by Morgen Chocolate.

Two children
looking at rabbit
over fence, Heris
#444, 6-1/2",
ca.1930. $450.

Angelic, four piece boy, Anton Reiche
#5289, 6-1/2", ca.1910. $350-$500.

Boy with bunnies, Heris #431, 4 1/8", ca.1930. $450.

Victorian child on rocking bunny,
Anton Reiche #6388, 4-1/2",
ca.1910. *Collection of Moni
Marceau.* $450 and up.

Girl riding elephant, Anton Reiche #13252, 4", ca.1930. *Collection and photo courtesy of William Timberlake M.D.* $450-$650.

Hansel, LeCerf #2188, 5", ca.1930. $175.

Hansel and Gretel at the witch's house, Walter #6091, 3-1/2", ca.1930. $350-$450.

Chocolate by Morgen Chocolate.

Gretel, LeCerf #2189, 5", ca.1930. $175.

The witch with Hansel and Gretel, Anton Reiche #28166, 4-1/2", ca.1930. *Collection of Diane Cazalet.* $350-$450.

Fairy tale scene of Hansel and Gretel outside witch's house, Walter #5330, 6-1/4", ca. 1930. *Collection of Paul and Fredricka Schwanka.* $500 and up.

Reverse.

Fairy tale scene of Snow White, Walter, also marked "import" #5335, 6", ca.1930. *Collection of Paul and Fredricka Schwanka.* $500 and up.

Reverse.

Humpty Dumpty, Walter, 6", ca.1930. *Collection of Rex Morgen.* $250-$350.

Fairy tale scene of two gnomes in an egg, Kutzscher #5046, 3", ca.1930. $350-$500.

Chocolate by Morgen Chocolate.

Beeswax figure and photo by Kathryn Campbell.

Little Red Riding Hood and wolf, Anton Reiche #8381, 3-1/2", ca.1920. $350-$450.

Cast mold of Little Red Riding Hood, 4", ca.1920. *Photo and Collection of Kathryn Campbell.* $250.

Vintage postcard.

Face, 5", ca.1930. *Collection of Monica Tinhofer.* $75.

Hansel and Gretel, Hörnlein #7002, 8-1/2", ca.1950. $150.

Happy face, 4", ca.1950. $50.

Sad face, 4", ca.1950. $50.

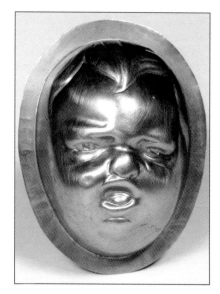

Odd egg face, 4", ca.1930. $75.

Chocolate by Morgen Chocolate.

Face, 5", ca.1930. $75.

Binche is a town in Belgium where people dress in elaborate costumes during Carnival and throw oranges to all the children in the crowd.

Stan Laurel, Bruning Meyer #5289, 6-3/4", ca.1940. $150-$250.

Gilles de Binche, Anton Reiche #30788, 7-1/2", ca.1920. *Collection of Diane Cazalet.* $350 and up.

Teddy Roosevelt, 5-1/2", ca.1930. $250.

Mystery man, Anton Reiche #13341,
6", ca.1920. $250.

Hat for scout, #5715.
*Collection of Paul and
Fredricka Schwanka.*

Scout, Anton Reiche #5715, 9-1/4", ca.1920. *Collection
of Paul and Fredricka Schwanka.* $350 and up.

Boxer, Létang #3722,
8-1/2", ca.1930.
*Collection of Diane
Cazalet.* $250.

Ranger, Anton Reiche
#16590, 6", ca.1920.
$200-$300.

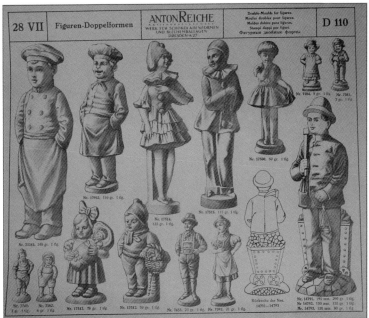

Page from original Anton Reiche catalog.

Boxer, Létang #3721, 8-1/2",
ca.1930. *Collection of Diane
Cazalet.* $250.

Coal miner, Anton Reiche
#14291, 7-1/2", ca.1920.
Collection of Carolyn Byrnes.
$250-$350.

Boy with dog in basket, Anton Reiche
#17512, 4-1/4", ca.1920. $250-$275.

Boy with bunny, Kutzscher
#13075, 5-1/2", ca.1920.
*Collection of Moni
Marceau.* $250-$350.

Chalkware and
photo courtesy of
Moni Marceau.

Chef, Anton Reiche #23345, 7-1/2",
ca.1920. *Collection of Diane Cazalet.*
$250-$350.

Children pulling egg, Anton Reiche #6808,
3", ca.1910. $250-$400.

Boy with toy hoop, Riecke
#4140, 5", ca.1930.
$175-$200.

Baker, Anton Reiche
#28805, 5-1/2",
ca.1920. *Collection of
Diane Cazalet.* $250.

142

Easter postcard.

Page from original
Kutzscher catalog.

Fine gentleman, 6-1/2", ca.1920. $200-$275.

Gentleman riding a bicycle,
Anton Reiche #7877, 4",
ca.1920. $250-$300.

Gentleman riding a bicycle, Anton Reiche #7871, 6", ca.1920. $250-$350.

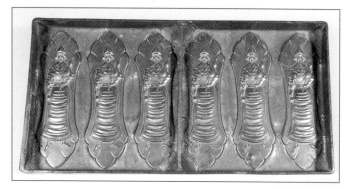

"Schwedin" flat, Riecke #5009, ca.1925.
Collection of Carolyn Byrnes. $250.

"Geisha" flat, Riecke # 5007, ca.1925.
Collection of Carolyn Byrnes. $250.

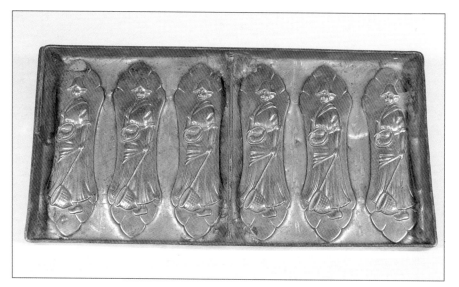

"Holländerin" flat, Riecke #5008, ca.1925.
Collection of Carolyn Byrnes. $250.

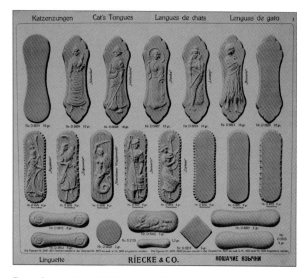

Page from original Riecke catalog.

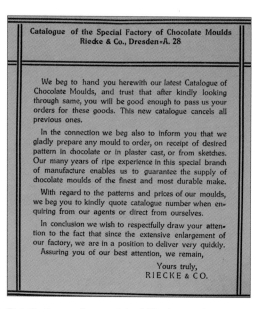

Detail of page from original Riecke catalog.

Bathing Belle, Anton
Reiche #17505, 7",
ca.1920. $350-$450.

Little swimmer, Anton Reiche, 5-1/2",
ca.1920. *Collection of Rex Morgen.*
$175-$250.

Beach chair beauty, Anton Reiche
#32846, 5", ca.1940. *Collection
of Carolyn Byrnes.* $250.

Bathing Barney, Anton
Reiche #17504, 5",
ca.1920. *Collection of
Diane Cazalet.* $250.

Advertising card for Huyler's Chocolate.

145

Various Frozen Charlotte dolls, Anton Reiche #7801, 7";
7802, 6"; & 7803, 5"; ca.1920. $175, $150, and $100.

Charlie Chaplin movie character, Anton
Reiche #20110, 7", ca.1930. *Collection
of Diane Cazalet.* $250-$400.

Boy in bathtub, Walter
#5406, 4-1/2",
ca.1930. $150.

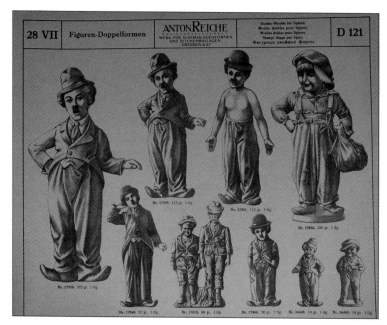

Page from original Anton Reiche catalog.

"Mutt & Jeff" characters, Anton
Reiche #17615, 5", ca.1920.
Collection of Diane Cazalet. $200.

146

Man with cigar, Anton Reiche, 6", ca.1930.
Collection of Diane Cazalet. $150.

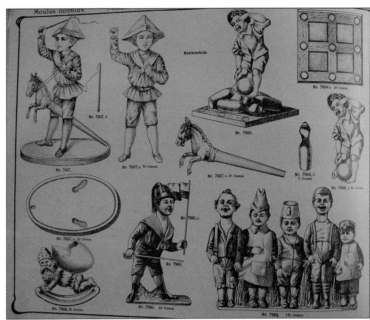

Page from original Anton Reiche catalog.
Collection of Monica Tinhofer.

Schoolgirl, Walter
#5284, 6",
ca.1920.
$150-$200.

Boy with cannon, Walter, 6", ca.1930. $250.

Boy with monkey, Anton Reiche #7552, 4-1/2". *Collection and photo courtesy of William Timberlake M.D.* $250-$350.

Angelic child with vase, Létang #2910, 7-1/2", ca.1920. $450 and up.

Victorian girl with wheat and sickle, Anton Reiche, 5", ca.1920. $250.

Mr. Peanut, 7". *Collection and photo courtesy of William Timberlake M.D.* $200 and up.

Angelic child with vase, Sommet, 7-1/2", ca.1920. The Létang and Sommet versions of this mold appear to be identical, yet have subtle differences. *Collection of Rex Morgen.* $450 and up.

Miniature couple, Anton Reiche #7536, 3-1/2", ca.1920. $250.

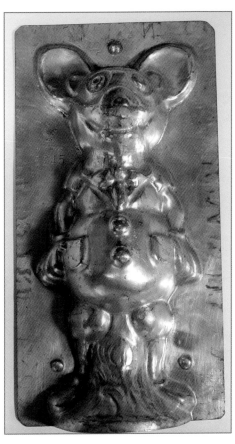

Minnie Mouse with tennis racket,
Anton Reiche, 5", ca.1930.
Collection of Diane Cazalet. $600
and up.

Donald Duck, Eppelsheimer
#8246, 10", ca.1930. *Collection of
Diane Cazalet.* $600 and up.

Mickey Mouse, Eppelsheimer
#8245, 10", ca.1930. *Collection of
Diane Cazalet.* $600 and up.

Mickey Mouse with
ball, Anton Reiche
#27121, 7",
ca.1930. *Collection
of Diane Cazalet.*
$600 and up.

Molds from Diane Cazalet on display at
the Copia Museum in Napa, California.

149

Donald Duck, Vormenfabriek #16358, 5", ca.1960. $150-$250.

Felix the Cat, Anton Reiche #13005, 5", ca.1920. *Collection of Diane Cazalet.* $450 and up.

Pig with harp, Anton Reiche #8588, 3-1/2", ca.1920. *Collection of Ginny Betourne.* $200-$250.

Mickey Mouse, Teich #3321, 4-1/2", ca.1930. $650 and up.

Felix the Cat walking, Anton Reiche #17601, 5-1/2", ca.1920. *Collection of Diane Cazalet.* $450 and up.

One of three little pigs, Anton Reiche #30943, 4-1/2", ca.1930. *Collection of Diane Cazalet.* $450 and up.

Two of three little pigs, Anton Reiche #30944, 4-1/2", ca.1930. *Collection of Diane Cazalet.* $450 and up.

Three of three little pigs, Anton Reiche #30945, 4-1/2", ca.1930. *Collection of Ginny Betourne.* $450 and up.

A different version of the three little pigs, Anton Reiche #29792, 5-1/2", ca.1930. *Collection of Ginny Betourne.* $450 and up.

Chalkware by Ginny Betourne.

Small dressed pig, Anton Reiche #32255, 3-3/4", ca.1940. *Collection of Ginny Betourne.* $150-$250.

151

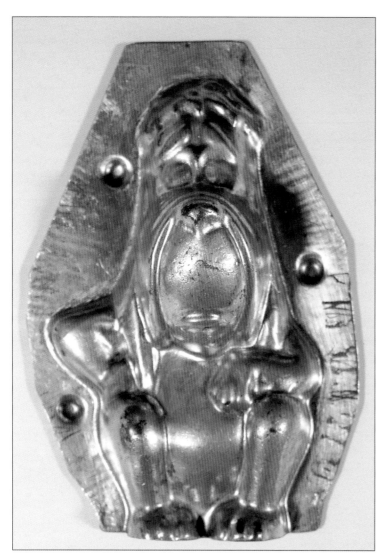

Droopy Dog cartoon character, 5-1/2",
ca.1950. *Collection of Diane Cazalet.* $250.

Preacher cat, Riecke, 4", ca.1930. $200-$250.

Mother Goose, Kutzscher
#13080, 4-1/2", ca.1920.
Collection of Diane Cazalet.
$350-$450.

Chalkware and photo courtesy of
Vaillancourt Folk Art.

King and Queen, Anton Reiche
#28107 & #28106, 7", ca.1930.
*Collection and photo courtesy of
Vaillancourt.* $250-$350 each.

153

Clowns

Chalkware by
Penny Burns.

Boy dressed as clown pointing to heart,
Anton Reiche #15538, 11-3/4", ca.1920.
Collection of Rex Morgen. $450-$600.

Chocolate by Morgen
Chocolate.

Clown with round moon, Anton Reiche
#5957, 9", ca.1920. *Collection of Moni
Marceau.* $450-$600.

Chalkware by Penny Burns.

Clown, Laurösch #4219, 11",
ca.1930. $450-$600.

Clown with pig on overalls, Anton Reiche
#27014, 5-3/4", ca.1920. *Collection of
Carolyn Byrnes.* $350-$450.

Rabbit in clown suit, Anton Reiche
#26420, 6-1/4", ca.1920. *Collection of
Monica Tinhofer.* $350-$450.

Child dressed as clown,
Anton Reiche #24915,
3", ca.1920. *Collection
of Diane Cazalet.* $200.

Page from
original
Laurösch
catalog.

Page from original
Anton Reiche catalog.

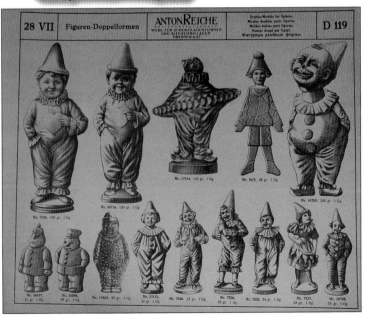

155

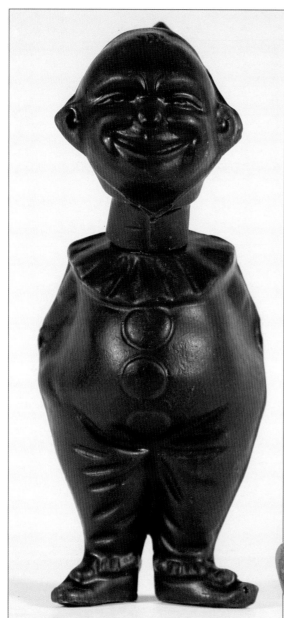

Detail of clown body, Anton Reiche #10785, 4-1/2", head 3-1/2", ca.1920. $550-$700.

Chocolate by Morgen Chocolate.

Mold detail.

Clowns riding pig, Anton Reiche #27114, 5-1/2",
ca.1930. *Collection of Ginny Betourne.* $450.

Clown in egg, Walter #2658, 3", ca.1930. $150.

Puppet, Anton Reiche #7675, ca.1910.
Collection of Rex Morgen. $250.

Cat dressed as clown, Anton Reiche
#24774, 4-1/2", ca.1920. $250-$350.

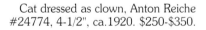

Clown breaking out of
egg, Walter #5852, 3",
ca.1950. *Collection of
Carolyn Byrnes.* $50.

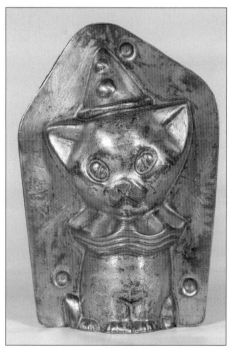

Halloween

Halloween is thought to have originated from the Celtic celebration in Ireland of "All Hallows Day" when all Saints in Heaven were honored. October 31 was the last day of the Celtic year and the day of "All Hallows Eve."

The Catholic Church celebrates "All Saints' Day" on November 1 as a remembrance of every martyr's death for Christ. Lutherans observe the day by remembering all saints both dead and living.

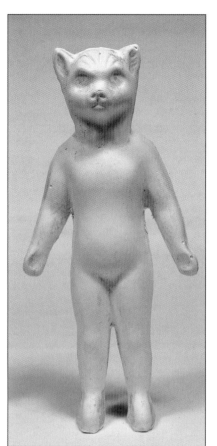

Unpainted chalkware.

Child with cat mask, 6", ca.1920. $450-$600.

"Ready for Trick or Treating,"
by EllesCreativeBrushworks.

Chalkware Halloween cat with chenille tail, by Ginny Betourne of Trout Creek Folk Art.

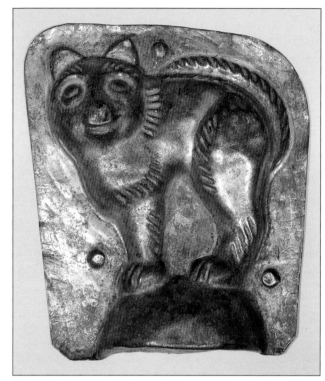

Thick arched cat, 4", ca.1930. *Collection of Diane Cazalet.* $350-$500.

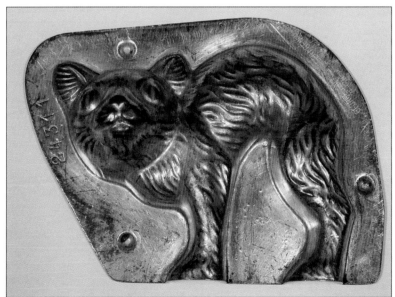

Arched cat, Anton Reiche #24311, 4", ca.1920. *Collection of Diane Cazalet.* $350-$500.

"The Pumpkin Man" by Susan Brack.

Scarecrow, Weygandt #443, 5", ca.1950.
Collection of Ginny Betourne. $300-$400.

Papier mâché scarecrow by Susan Brack.

Jack o' Lantern, Eppelsheimer #7400, 2" ca. 1940.

Chalkware waiting to be painted at Vaillancourt Folk Art.

Chocolate by Morgen Chocolate.

Chalkware by Penny Burns.

Witch riding broom with owl, Walters #8433, 4", ca.1920. *Collection of Rex Morgen*. $500 and up.

Witch riding broom with owl, Walters #8465, 5", ca.1920. *Collection of Ginny Betourne*. $500 and up.

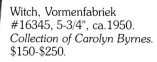

Witch, Vormenfabriek #16345, 5-3/4", ca.1950. *Collection of Carolyn Byrnes*. $150-$250.

161

Barley candy witch by Dorothy
Timberlake Candies.

Witch on broom,
Eppelsheimer #8011, 6",
ca.1930. *Collection of Ginny
Betourne.* $250-$350.

Chalkware by Ginny
Betourne.

Witch on broom, Anton Reiche #25341, 3-3/4",
ca.1920. *Collection of Ginny Betourne.* $650 and up.

Jack o' Lantern,
Weygandt #403,
3-1/4", ca.1950.
*Collection of
Ginny Betourne.*
$200-250.

Chalkware by
Penny Burns.

"Look out below," by Susan Brack.

Chalkware by Penny Burns.

Jack O' Lantern, Anton Reiche
#17688, 1-3/4", ca.1920.
Collection of Ginny Betourne.
$250-$300.

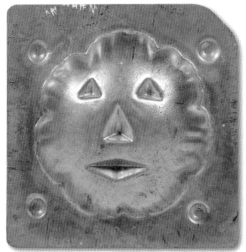

Jack O' Lantern, Walter and Van Emden NY,
2-1/2", ca.1930. *Collection of Ginny
Betourne.* $200-$300.

Page from original Anton
Reiche catalog.

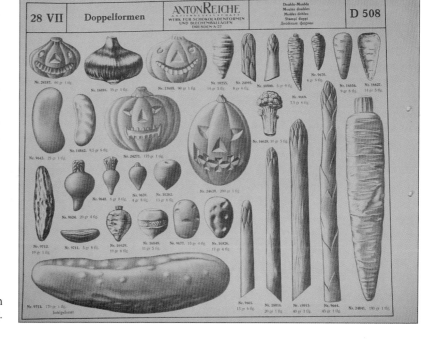

Chalkware by Penny Burns.

Jack O' Lantern, Eppelsheimer #8078, 3-1/4", ca.1930. *Collection of Ginny Betourne.* $250-$350.

Chocolate Jack O' Lantern's at Morgen Chocolate.

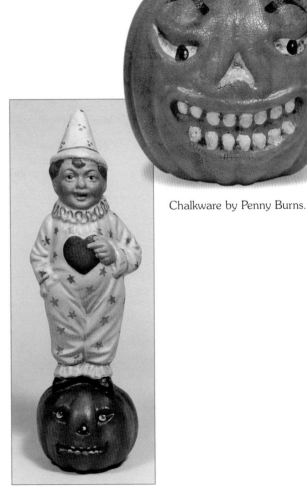

Jack O' Lantern, ca.1950. *Collection of Ginny Betourne.* $150-$200.

Chalkware by Penny Burns.

Chalkware by Penny Burns.

Chalkware by Penny Burns.

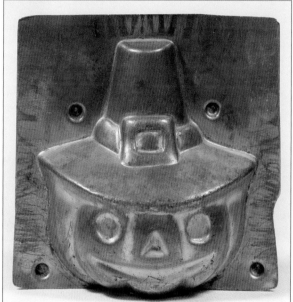

Jack O' Lantern in hat, Weygandt #432, 3-1/2", ca.1950. *Collection of Ginny Betourne.* $250-$350.

Chalkware by Penny Burns.

Chalkware by Ginny Betourne.

Cats with mice on tails, Walter, ca.1930. $150 & $175.

Witch, Laurösch #3042, 5-1/2",
ca.1950. *Collection of Ginny
Betourne.* $175-$250.

Unpainted chalkware
courtesy of Penny Burns.

Chalkware by Penny Burns.

Laughing tomcat,
Anton Reiche #17492,
4", ca.1920. $250.

Side view of
witch.

Page from the Willi Thormeier Magdeburg catalog of 1936, showing witch with Hansel and Gretel.

166

Art Deco cat, Hörnlein #2551, 5-1/2",
ca.1940. $350.

In Italy on January 6, children eagerly anticipate the arrival of the good witch of the Epiphany La Befana, who enters chimneys and fills the shoes of the well-behaved children with treats; appropriately coal is left in the shoes of the children who have misbehaved.

Coven of witches, Germany #1248, 6", ca.1930.
Collection of Ginny Betourne. $800 and up.

Halloween
postcard.

Cat on pumpkin, Weygandt #145,
5-1/4", ca.1950. *Collection of
Kathryn Campbell.* $200-$250.

Chalkware by
Ginny
Betourne.

Chalkware by Kathryn
Campbell.

167

Krampus

In Austria, a strange and frightening creature called Krampus is usually associated with Christmas and arrives with St. Nicholas. Krampus is a devilish figure, often in chains and dressed in fur with a scary mask and a long red tongue. Krampus carries switches and clubs to threaten children who misbehave. St. Nicholas never allows Krampus to harm any of the children.

Krampus with cape, 9-1/2", ca.1930. *Collection of Monica Tinhofer.* $350 and up.

Krampus head, 6", ca.1930. *Collection of Monica Tinhofer.* $450 and up.

Olympic Krampus, 5", ca.1930. *Collection of Ginny Betourne.* $350-$500.

Krampus on motorcycle, Laurösch #4537, 5-1/2", ca.1930. *Collection of Monica Tinhofer.* $350 and up.

Krampus, Obermann, 4", ca.1930. *Collection of Ginny Betourne.* $200-$250.

Chalkware by Penny Burns.

Page from original Anton Reiche catalog.

Krampus, 4", ca.1930. *Collection of Ginny Betourne.* $250-$350.

Barley candy Krampus sucker, courtesy of Dorothy Timberlake Candies.

Flute player Krampus, 6", ca.1920. *Collection of Ginny Betourne.* $600 and up.

Krampus face, #3552, 5-1/4", ca.1930.
Collection of Monica Tinhofer. $350 and up.

Neptune Krampus, #1245, 6", ca.1930.
Collection of Diane Cazalet. $600 and up.

Vintage Krampus die cut.

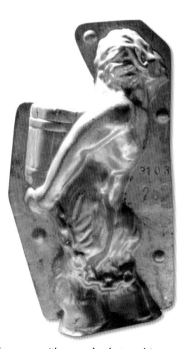

Krampus with open basket on his
back, #3103, 7", ca.1930. *Collection
of Monica Tinhofer.* $350 and up.

Krampus with basket, 7", ca.1930. $450.

Krampus holding chains, 6", ca.1920.
Collection of Monica Tinhofer. $250-$350.

Krampus flat, Anton Reiche, 8", ca.1930. $250.

Krampus with switch, 6", ca.1920. *Collection of Diane Cazalet.* $250-$350.

Chalkware by Penny Burns.

Krampus with switch, #160, 5", ca.1930. *Collection of Ginny Betourne.* $350-$400.

Vintage Krampus die cut.

Krampus playing flute,
#1246, ca.1920.
*Collection of Ginny
Betourne.* $350 and up.

Krampus with club and
chains, 5", ca.1940. $200.

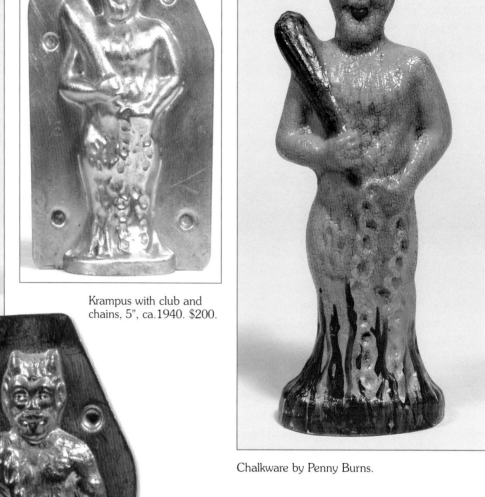

Chalkware by Penny Burns.

Little Krampus,
JOH.FOHN #88, 4",
ca.1930. *Collection of
Ginny Betourne.* $175.

Krampus in cowboy boot, 5-1/2",
ca.1930. *Collection of Ginny
Betourne.* $450 and up.

Santas

As Dutch settlers from Amsterdam came to New York City during the early 1800s, they brought "Sinter Klaas" with them, a legendary figure who looked like a bishop and rode a white horse as he filled children's shoes with candy on December 6. Americans mispronouncing Sinter Klaas created Santa Claus, who became the jolly and plump gift-giver from the North Pole with a sleigh pulled by reindeer.

Santa face in chalkware by Anne Launius.

Extremely rare Santa face, Anton Reiche, 6" wide x 12" long , ca.1920. $5,000 and up.

Detail of Santa face.

Anton Reiche chocolate mold advertisement. *Collection of Erwin and Monika Gschwind.*

Body to Santa face shown on previous page, Anton Reiche #11166, 23", ca.1920. *Collection of Vaillancourt Folk Art.* $3,000 and up.

Large classic Santa, Anton Reiche # 21335, 36" tall, ca.1930. *Collection and Photo courtesy of Erwin and Monika Gschwind.* $10,000 and up.

174

In 1863, Thomas Nast, a political cartoonist began a series of annual drawings in *Harper's Weekly* based on the Santa descriptions found in Washington Irving's work and Clement Clark Moore's poem "The Night Before Christmas."

"Thomas Nast" style Santa, Anton Reiche #17571, 8", ca.1920. *Collection of Rex Morgen.* $450-$650.

Santa, Anton Reiche #21122, 6", ca.1920. $350-$450.

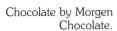

Chocolate by Morgen Chocolate.

Santa, Anton Reiche #17574, 3-3/4", ca.1920. $250.

175

Santa with toys and elephant, Anton Reiche #21120, 10", ca.1920. $700-$850.

Santa with bag and separate arm, Anton Reiche, ca.1920. *Collection and photo courtesy of Erwin and Monika Gschwind.* $1,500 and up.

Chalkware by Moni Marceau.

Santa with bag and Christmas tree, Anton Reiche. *Collection and photo courtesy of Bruce and Lorry Hanes of Dad's Follies.*

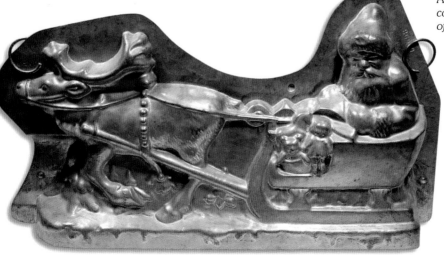

Santa and sleigh, Anton Reiche #26980, 10" tall x 18" long, ca.1920. *Collection of Diane Cazalet.* $5,000 and up.

"The Enchanted Sleigh," by Susan Brack.

Santa and sleigh, Anton Reiche #27620, 4", ca.1920. $450-$700.

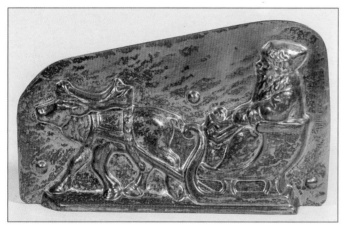

Santa and sleigh, Anton Reiche #24445, 7", ca.1920. $750-$900.

Chocolate by Morgen Chocolate.

Chocolate Santas waiting to be trimmed at Morgen Chocolate.

Santa and sleigh, Jaburg #099, 8", ca.1920. *Collection of Paul and Fredricka Schwanka.* $750-$850.

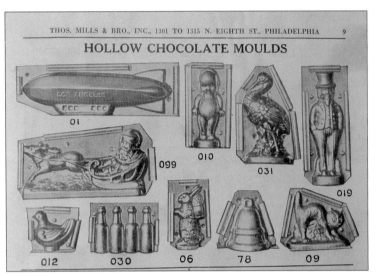

THOS. MILLS & BRO., INC., 1301 TO 1315 N. EIGHTH ST., PHILADELPHIA   9

HOLLOW CHOCOLATE MOULDS

Page from original Jaburg catalog.

Design details of Santa.

Santa with toy horse and rider in satchel, Heris #171, 11", ca.1920. *Collection of Diane Cazalet.* $900 and up.

178

Chalkware at Vaillancourt Folk Art.

Santa with little girl, Anton Reiche #32821, 5",
ca.1920. *Collection of Moni Marceau.* $650-$950.

Santa with kids in bag, Heris #4042, 7", ca.1930.
Collection of Moni Marceau. $650-$850.

Chalkware and photo courtesy
of Moni Marceau.

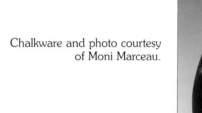

Santa on motorcycle, Heris
#186, 6", ca.1930. *Collec-
tion and photo courtesy of
Erwin and Monika Gschwind.*
$350-$500.

Santa on motorcycle, Laurösch #4165, 6", ca.1930. *Collection of Diane Cazalet.* $350-$500.

Santa rider and motorcycle, Walter, Santa #8442, 5", ca.1920. Motorcycle #8438, 6-1/4", ca.1920. (See the character section for the male and female rider in this series.) $650-$800.

Karl Pauli advertisement ca.1930.

Page from original Kutzscher catalog.

Chocolate by Morgen Chocolate.

Santa with teddy bear and lantern, Kutzscher #13133, 14", ca.1920. *Collection of Rex Morgen.* $2,000 and up.

Gnome advertising chocolate.

Gnome, Anton Reiche #20182, 2-1/2",
ca.1920. *Collection of Ginny Betourne.* $250.

Chalkware by
Ginny Betourne.

Gnome, Obermann #8213,
3", ca.1930. $250.

Gnome, #9, 3",
ca.1920. $150-$250.

Chunky gnome, Anton Reiche
#30749, 4-1/2", ca.1920. $250.

Gnome, 3-3/4",
ca.1930. $250.

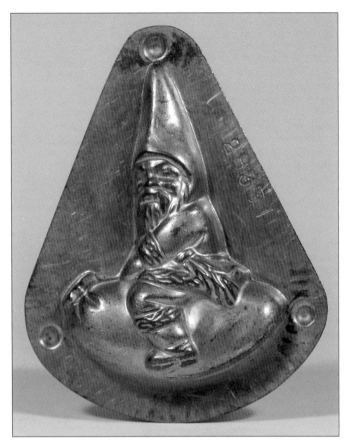

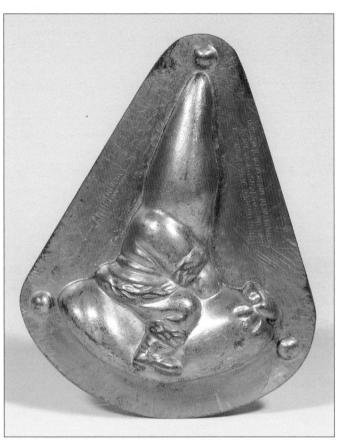

Gnome riding bag, Anton Reiche #28331, 3-1/2", ca.1930. *Collection of Kathryn Campbell.* $300-$450.

Detail of reverse.

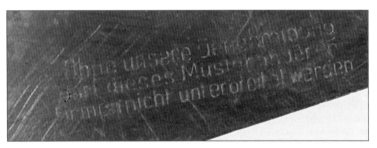

Unusual marking on an Anton Reiche mold, from the back of this Santa. Translated by Moni Marceau, it reads: *"Do not copy this sample without permission from the manufacturer."*

Gnomes carrying pinecone, Walter #9878, 5", ca.1930. *Collection of Wendy Stys-Van Eimeren.* $200-$300.

Beeswax casting by Kathryn Campbell.

Gnome on mushroom, Walter #9888, 4", ca.1930. *Collection of Wendy Stys-Van Eimeren.* $250-$350.

"Polar Express," by Susan Brack.

Chalkware by Wendy Stys-Van Eimeren.

Star Santa, Anton Reiche #30781, 9-1/2", ca.1930. *Collection of Paul and Fredricka Schwanka.* $1,500 and up.

Christmas cards made from Anton Reiche chocolate mold designs by Rita Reiche. The cards are made by pressing foil paper into a handmade replica of an original mold.

Reproduced from original chocolate mould manufactured by the Anton Reiche Chocolate Factory

Exclusive Design from

ANTON REICHE
DRESDEN

SCHUTZ·MARKE   MARQUE DÉPOSÉE

Chocolate Mould Factory

World's largest and most famous chocolate mould factory

Dresden, Germany
1870-1950

© 1997 by Reiche Ltd.

Santa riding shooting star, Matfer, Made in France, 9-1/2", ca.1950. *Collection of Susan Brack.* $450-$500.

Papier mâché by Susan Brack.

Santa with donkey and angel, Anton Reiche #6856, 4-1/2",
ca.1910. *Collection of Anne Launius.* $800 and up.

Page from original Kutzscher catalog.

Santa with deer, Kutzscher #13099, 6", ca.1920.
Collection of Moni Marceau. $800 and up.

Chalkware at Vaillancourt Folk Art.

Santa riding donkey, Anton Reiche, 6-1/2", ca.1920.
Collection of Moni Marceau. $250-$300.

Santa riding donkey with special opening for tree,
Anton Reiche #6634, 5", ca.1910. $250-$350.

"Zonkey" in papier mâché and photo by Susan Brack.

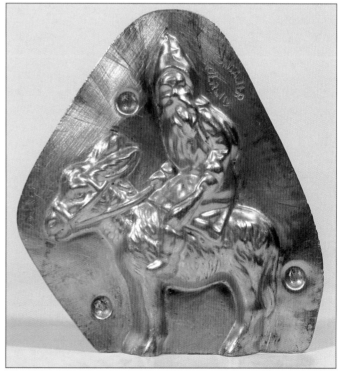

Mini Santa on donkey with switch, Walter
#2607, 3-1/2", ca.1920. $200-$250.

Mini Santa on donkey, Anton Reiche #6854, 3-1/2", ca.1910. $200-$250.

Art Deco Santa with tree and bear, Laurösch #3030, 5-1/2", ca.1930. $450-$600.

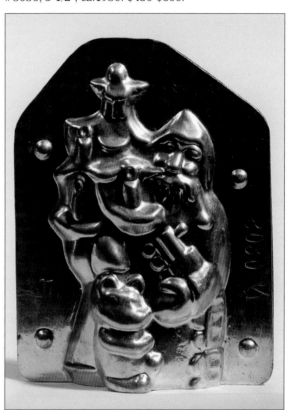

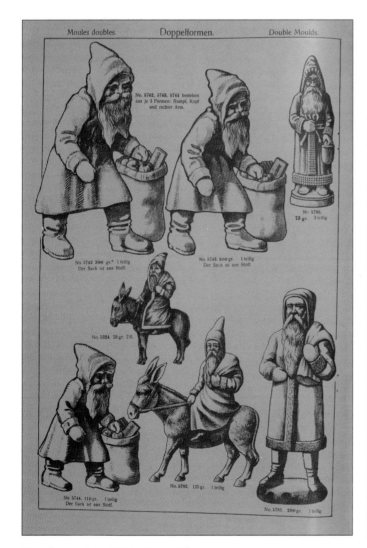

Page from original Kutzscher catalog.

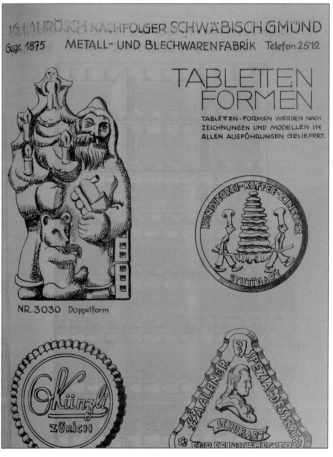

Page from original Laurösch catalog.

Kutzscher was a German mold manufacturer in business for less than thirty years, from 1900-1929. The Kutzscher artists had a whimsical style and wonderful original designs, producing molds with excellent detail. Kutzscher molds were rarely marked so they are often mistaken for Anton Reiche molds.

Santa riding pig, Kutzscher #5539, 3-1/2", ca.1920. $650 and up.

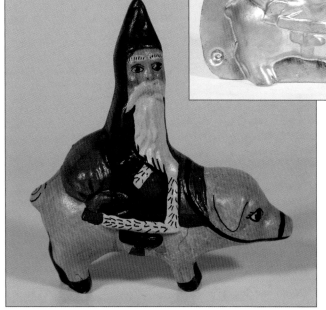

Chalkware by Vaillancourt Folk Art.

Chalkware by Anne Launius.

Page from Kutzscher catalog showing three sizes of Santa riding pig.

Santa riding pig, 5", Kutzscher, ca.1920. *Collection of Anne Launius.* $650 and up.

Santa with tree, Anton Reiche #1559, *Collection of Diane Cazalet.* $700 and up.

Santa with tree, Anton Reiche #26904, 4-1/2", ca.1930. *Collection of Wendy Stys-Van Eimeren.* $500-$650.

Chalkware by Wendy Stys-Van Eimeren at Pineberrylane.com.

Vintage postcard.

Santa with tree, 10-3/4", ca.1930. *Collection of Moni Marceau.* $800 and up.

Santa with tree, Hörnlein
#1015, 7-1/2", ca.1940.
Collection of Carolyn Byrnes.
$350-$450.

Chalkware by Penny Burns.

Postcard style mold of
Santa with children,
Anton Reiche #518, 8",
ca.1920. $800 and up.

Vintage postcard.

Chocolate by
Morgen
Chocolate.

Little Santa with large tree,
Leon Létang #11435, 7",
ca.1920. *Collection of Rex
Morgen.* $650 and up.

190

St. Nick is the special saint to children. According to legend, he arrives on donkey, horse, or simply walking on December 5 or 6 dressed as a bishop. In some countries, St. Nick travels with angels or other companions, variously known as Zwarte Piet, Krampus or Ruprecht.

St. Nick, #64, 11", ca.1930. *Collection of Monica Tinhofer*. $500.

St. Nick, Anton Reiche #26308, 3", ca.1920. $150.

St. Nick, 4", ca.1930. $150.

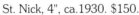

St. Nick head, 6-3/4", ca.1920. *Collection of Monica Tinhofer*. $350 and up.

St. Nick with Bible, Joh. Fohn, 6-1/2", ca.1930. $250.

Vintage St. Nick die cut.

Papier mâché St. Nick and photo by Susan Brack.

St. Nick with three kids, #4993, 9-1/2", ca.1930. $250.

St. Nick with bag, Hörnlein #1016, 10-1/2", ca.1940. $500.

St. Nick on horse, Anton Reiche #29244, 6", ca.1930. *Collection of Diane Cazalet.* $350.

Art Deco St. Nick, Teich #4031, 6", ca.1930. $350-$450.

Zwarte Piet is a Christmas icon in the Netherlands who acts as a helper to Sinterklaas (the Dutch name for St. Nicholas). The Piets are extremely popular and are seen as being playful and merry. St. Nick is serious with the children asking about their behavior and giving them fruit, while it is the Piets who hand out treats and candy.

Peter, St. Nick's assistant, Vormenfabriek #15929, 7", ca.1950. $150.

Vintage postcard showing St. Nick and his assistant Peter (also known as Zwarte Piet).

St. Nick, Teich #4320, 4-1/2", ca.1930. $200-$250.

St. Nick, Teich, 7-1/2", ca.1930. $250-$400.

Vintage ink blotter advertising molded chocolate figures made from the Vormen molds on next page.

St. Nick, Vormen #15245, 7",
ca.1950. $100.

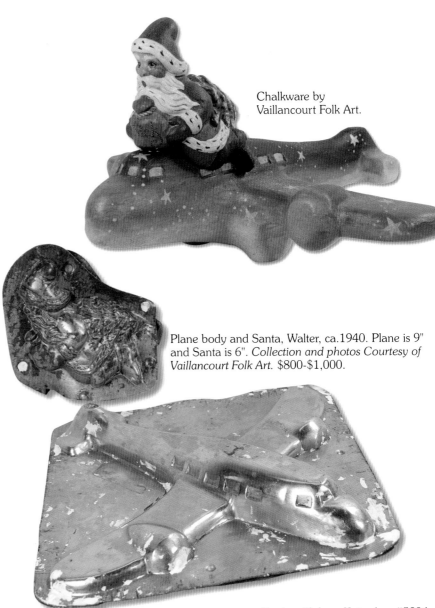

Chalkware by
Vaillancourt Folk Art.

Plane body and Santa, Walter, ca.1940. Plane is 9"
and Santa is 6". *Collection and photos Courtesy of
Vaillancourt Folk Art.* $800-$1,000.

Santa, Vormen #16144, 4",
ca.1950. $150.

Page from original Kutzscher catalog.

Santa with bag, Kutzscher #5234,
10", ca.1910. $650-$800.

Art Deco Santa, Létang #4284, 6-1/2",
ca.1930. $350-$450.

Front view.

Russian style Santa, Kutzscher, 10",
ca.1910. $800 and up.

Chalkware at Vaillancourt Folk Art.

Vintage photo of Moni Marceau and her
mother in Germany with chocolate Santa.

Chalkware and photo courtesy of Moni's Folkart.

Hiking Santa, Weygandt, 12-1/2", ca.1940. $800 and up.

Punch card advertising
chocolate hiking Santa.

Santa and helper on sled, Kutzscher #5614, 4", ca.1910.
Collection of Paul and Fredricka Schwanka. $650 and up.

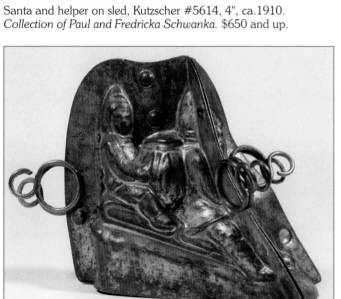

Additional view.

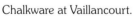

Chalkware at Vaillancourt.

Santa and elf with sled, Heris #181, 9", ca.1930.
Collection of Moni Marceau. $800 and up.

Chalkware and photo courtesy of Moni's Folkart.

Tall Santa, Heris #4179, 9-1/4", ca.1930. $350.

Santa with button coat, #13308, 6",
ca.1910. $350-$450.

Button coat Santa with puppet on back,
#1472, 7", ca.1950. $200.

Back detail.

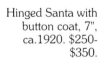

Hinged Santa with
button coat, 7",
ca.1920. $250-
$350.

Santa with satchel of
fruit, #2157, 7",
ca.1950. *Collection of
Carolyn Byrnes.* $250-
$300.

Santa with children postcard style mold, Anton Reiche #10399, 5" x 7". $800 and up.

Chocolate by Morgen Chocolate.

Children under tree post card style mold, Anton Reiche, 7", ca.1920. $650 and up.

Santa, Anton Reiche #27745, 10", ca.1920. $1,000 and up.

"Bear Tracks," by Susan Brack.

199

Modern Santa, Hörnlein #1055, 20",
ca.1950. *Collection of Ginny Betourne.*
$800 and up.

Papier mâché in progress by Ginny
Betourne.

Santa with satchel, Obermann,
12-1/2", ca.1920. *Collection of
Monica Tinhofer.* $800 and up.

Santa, Obermann, 7", ca.1920.
Collection of Ginny Betourne.
$350-$500.

Finished papier
mâché by Ginny
Betourne.

Cast aluminum, *extremely detailed Santa*, 11", can be used for chocolate, hard candy and chalkware. $800 and up.

Back detail.

Santa with satchel of fruit, Obermann, 9-1/2", ca.1920. *Collection of Monica Tinhofer.* $350-$400.

Papier mâché Santa by Susan Brack.

Santa at chimney, Létang #4964, 10", ca.1930. *Collection of Susan Brack.* $800 and up.

Heavy strip mold, Erich Bonck* #10384, 12", ca.1950. *Collection of Carolyn Byrnes.* $150.
*Son and nephew of Hermann Walter, using a pseudonym for business name; for more information on manufacturers and distributors *see* Carolyn Byrnes' new reference chart.

Face detail.

Santa, Heris #175, 10",
ca.1930. $600-$750.

Chalkware and
photo by
Moni's Folkart.

Chocolate by Morgen Chocolate.

Anton Reiche advertisement. *Collection and photo by Erwin and Monika Gschwind.*

Mini Santa with satchel, #26, 3-3/4", ca.1920. $150-$200.

Santa with satchel, 5", ca.1930. $200-$250.

Yellow ware by Kathryn Campbell.

The term Belsnickel came from Americans hearing German immigrants saying the word Pelznichol, which was the German name for Nicholas wearing fur or a pelt. Americans thought the Germans were saying Belsnickel and didn't know it meant that the Santa had fur. The term eventually evolved into a name representing a stern looking Santa with his hands in a muff.

Belsnickel style Santa, Anton Reiche, #25855, 6", ca.1930. $250-$300.

Mini Santa with tree, #7852,
ca.1910. *Collection of Ginny
Betourne.*
$450-$650.

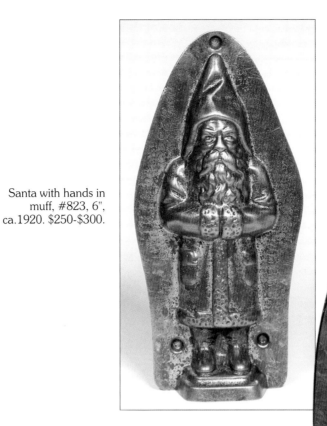

Santa with hands in
muff, #823, 6",
ca.1920. $250-$300.

Vintage postcard.

Santa with bag and
switch, 8", ca.1930.
*Collection of Carolyn
Deschenes.* $200-$300.

Chalkware by Carolyn
Deschenes.

Santa with
satchel, #4186,
7", ca.1930.
$300-$450.

Santa with tree and basket postcard style mold, Heris, 5-1/2" x 3-1/2", ca.1930. *Collection of Carolyn Byrnes.* $600 and up.

Santa with tree postcard style mold, Anton Reiche #520, 5" x 3-1/2", ca.1920. *Collection of Carolyn Byrnes.* $700 and up.

Chocolate by Robert Twardzik. Photo by Marcus Pinto.

Chocolate by Robert Twardzik. Photo by Marcus Pinto.

205

"Northern Lights," by Susan Brack.

Santa with bag, #28812, ca.1920.
Collection of Diane Cazalet. $650 and up.

Santa with shoe sled, #4765, 5", ca.1930.
Collection of Diane Cazalet. $450-$600.

In Sweden, a gnome named Juletomten delivers gifts in a sleigh pulled by goats.

Russian style hiking Santa, Anton Reiche #17584, 5",
ca.1920. *Collection of Diane Cazalet.* $650-$850.

Gnome with lantern,
6", ca.1920. *Collection of Monica Tinhofer.* $250-$350.

Gnome, Anton Reiche #22731, 6-1/2", ca.1920. $450-$600.

Gnome riding snail, #2247, 4", ca.1930. *Collection and photo courtesy of Vaillancourt Folk Art.* $250-$300.

Chalkware and photo courtesy of Vaillancourt Folk Art.

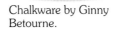
Chalkware by Ginny Betourne.

Gnome playing accordion, #4002, 6-1/2", ca.1920. *Collection of Ginny Betourne.* $250-$300.

207

Small gnome, Walter #9290, 3",
ca.1930. *Collection of Wendy
Stys-Van Eimeren.* $200-$300.

Chalkware by Wendy
Stys-Van Eimeren.

Santa, 4-1/4",
ca.1910. $200-
$300.

Chalkware and
photo by Diane
Cheffy.

Santa, Kutzscher #5511,
4-1/2", ca.1920. $200-
$300.

Page from original
Kutzscher catalog.

Santa with lantern, 8",
ca.1920. $350-$500.

Unpainted chalkware.

Father Christmas, Walter #5320, 20-1/4", ca.1920. $6,000 and up.

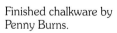

Page from Walter catalog.

Santa, Walter #2605, 4-1/2", ca.1920. $150-$250.

Finished chalkware by Penny Burns.

"St. Nick and the Snow Owl,"
by Susan Brack.

Santa driving Jag, Hörnlein #1023,
11", ca.1940. $600-$750.

Chalkware and photo
courtesy of Moni's Folkart.

Santa driving car, Heris #4180, 7", ca.1930. $250-$300.

Santa on sleigh with bag and puppet,
Anton Reiche #16730, 4-1/2", ca.1920.
$650 and up.

Chocolate by Morgen
Chocolate.

Santa on sleigh with Angel helpers, Kutzscher #5042, 3-1/2", ca.1910. $650 and up.

Santa at chimney, Eppelsheimer #6741, 4-1/2", ca.1920. *Collection of Diane Cazalet. $350-$500.*

Page from original Kutzscher catalog.

Papier mâché Santa and photo by Susan Brack.

Vintage Bunte Chocolate Santa Box.

Gathering of Santas. *Collection of The Dorchy Family.*

Art Deco Santa, 4", ca.1940.
$200-$250.

Chalkware by Carolyn
Deschenes.

Santa, Anton Reiche
#7843, 4", ca.1920.
*Collection of Carolyn
Deschenes.* $350-$600.

Santa with hands in muff, "Mayer
Hirschler" (name of distributor)
marked on mold, 3", ca.1920.
$175-$250.

Belsnickel style Santa,
Laurösch #3020, 4-1/2",
ca.1940. $125-$150.

Belsnickel style Santa,
Laurösch #3019, 3-3/4",
ca.1940. $125-$150.

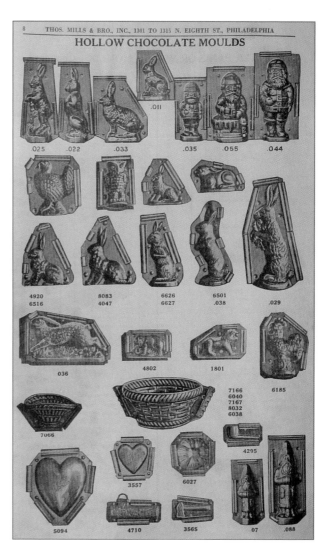

Page from original Jaburg catalog.

Chalkware and photo courtesy
of Moni's Folkart.

Santa with stick and bag,
Létang #4356, ca.1930.
*Collection and photo courtesy
of Moni's Folkart.* $350-$500.

Santa, Jaburg #7,
5-1/4", solid nickel
silver, ca.1930.
$200-$250.

213

American style Santa, Obermann, 4",
ca.1920. Obermann manufactured molds
in Budapest and Vienna. $175-$250.

Page from the Willi Thormeier Magdeburg catalog of 1936.

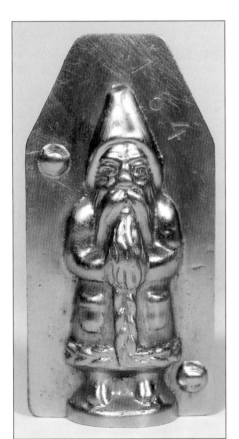

Mini Santa, Heris #164, 2-1/2", ca.1940.
Collection of Patrick Mullen. $150-$200.

Santa with hands in muff, Heris #166,
4-1/2", ca.1940. $150-$200.

Santa, Heris #166, 4-3/4", ca.1940. $150-
$200. Both of these Santas are marked
with the same Heris #166, however, they
are slightly different designs.

"A Winter's Ride," by Susan Brack.

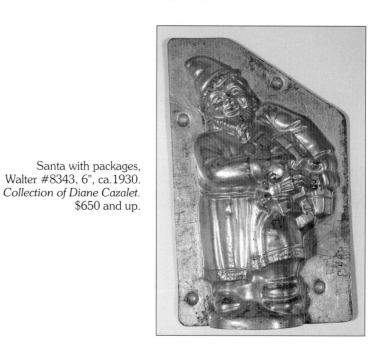

Santa with packages,
Walter #8343, 6", ca.1930.
Collection of Diane Cazalet.
$650 and up.

Papier mâché by Ginny Betourne.

Walking Santa, Hörnlein #1019, 18", ca.1950.
Collection of Ginny Betourne. $3,000 and up.

215

Santa,
Eppelsheimer
#8139, 7",
ca.1930. *Collection
of Diane Cazalet.*
$250-$300.

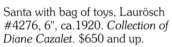

Santa with bag of toys, Laurösch
#4276, 6", ca.1920. *Collection of
Diane Cazalet.* $650 and up.

Detail of mold and
flange style.

Art Deco Santa with tree, 8-1/2", ca.1930.
Collection of Diane Cazalet. $800 and up.

Chalkware and photo
by Diane Cheffy.

Santa with bear in bag,
#1474, 4 3/4", ca.1930.
$200-$250.

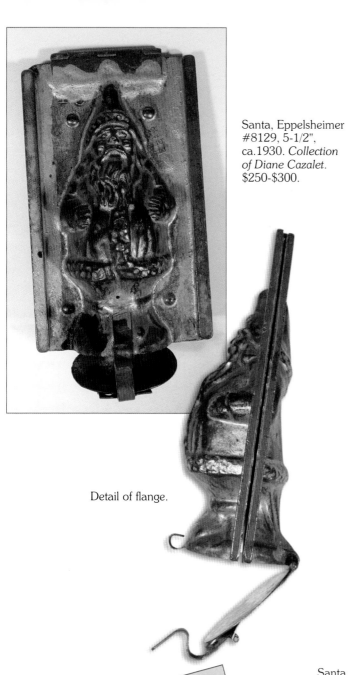

Santa, Eppelsheimer #8129, 5-1/2", ca.1930. *Collection of Diane Cazalet.* $250-$300.

Detail of flange.

Santa with angel helper, Anton Reiche #17576, 5-1/2", ca.1920. *Collection of Diane Cazalet.* $800 and up.

Santa with helper, Laurösch #4267, ca.1920. *Collection of Diane Cazalet.* $800 and up.

Vintage postcard.

Chalkware and photo by Moni's Folkart.

Santa with angel baker, Walter #5320, 5", ca.1910. *Collection of The Schwanka Family.* $800 and up.

Banquet ice cream mold, Eppelsheimer #194, 11". Ice cream molds can also be used for chocolate, beeswax, and chalkware. *Collection of Rex Morgen.* $800 and up.

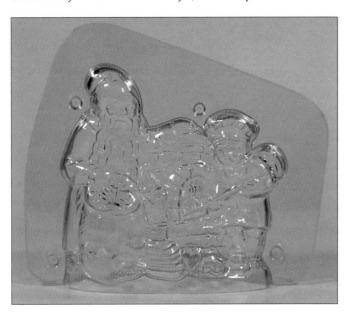

Chocolate by Morgen Chocolate.

Plastic copy of same mold.

Three-quarter-body Santa mold,
Randle & Smith England, 4-1/2",
ca.1940. $250-$300.

Finished chalkware at
Vaillancourt Folk Art.

Drawing from original
Laurösch catalog.

Nr. 3026 450 g 1teilig

Santa, Anton Reiche #16577,
4-1/2", ca.1920. $250-$350.

Serious Santa, 9"
ca.1930. $200-$250.

Little Santa, Anton Reiche
#7854, 4-1/2", ca.1910.
$300-$400.

Chalkware and photo
by Diane Cheffy.

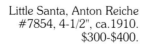

219

Santa, Weygandt #219, ca.1940. *Collection of Diane Cazalet.* $150-$200.

Santa with girl, Made in Germany #180, 7", ca.1930. *Collection of Moni Marceau.* $800 and up.

Tiny Santa, Anton Reiche #7846, 3-1/2", ca.1910. $300-$400.

Santa, Anton Reiche #6845, 6", ca.1910. $350-$500.

Tiny Santa, Laurösch #5357, 3-1/4", ca.1920. $250-$350.

Chalkware and photo courtesy of Moni's Folkart.

Chalkware by Penny Burns.

Fisherman Santa, Obermann #2087, 8-1/2", ca.1920. $800 and up.

Chalkware by Penny Burns.

Santa standing on snowball, #990, 6-1/4", ca.1920. $200-$250.

Santa with satchel, Anton Reiche #6850, 3-1/2", ca.1910. $150-$250.

"Toys From Above," by Susan Brack.

221

Santa with cape, Laurösch #3031, 6", ca.1930. *Collection of Diane Cazalet*. $450 and up.

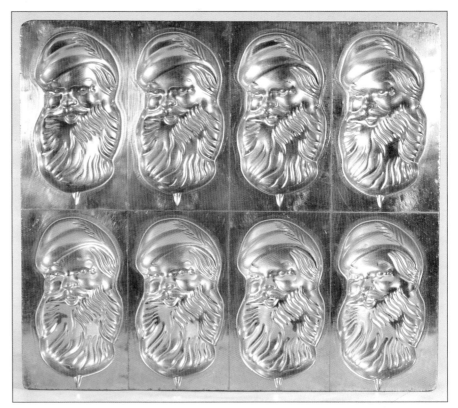

Santa Faces, chocolate sucker mold, 14-1/2" x 12-1/2", ca.1930. $350-$400.

Santa faces, Made in Germany #4018, 9-1/2", ca.1930. $250.

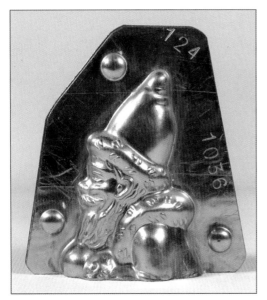

Santa head, #1036, 3-1/4", ca.1940. *Collection of Diane Cazalet*. $150-$200.

Classic Santa, Anton Reiche #24092, 5-1/2", ca.1920. $250-$300.

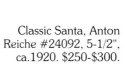

Santa with bag, 10", #979, ca.1920.
Collection of Moni Marceau. $650 and up.

Santa, Létang #3618, 10",
ca.1920. *Collection of
Diane Cazalet.* $250-$300.

Santa with tree, Anton Reiche,
#7918, 3-1/2", ca.1910. $400-$500.

Santas at Vaillancourt.

Skinny Santa with switch in
bag, Walter #9473, 7-1/4",
ca.1920. $250-$300.

Santa hands in muff, Riecke #257,
6-1/4", ca.1920. $200-$250.

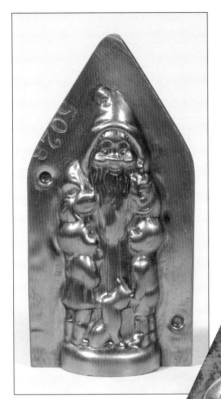

Santa with children and dog, Létang #5028, 4-1/4", ca.1950. $250-$300.

Chocolate by Morgen Chocolate.

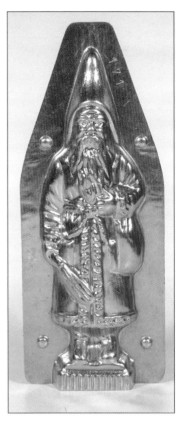

Santa with switch, Heris #171, 7-3/4", ca.1920. $175-$200.

Santa, Walter #5319, 14", ca.1920. *Collection of Rex Morgen.* $1,500 and up.

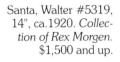

Santa with satchel and switch, Anton Reiche #30503 5" ca.1940. $250-$350.

Chalkware and photo by Diane Cheffy.

Santa with puppet, Hörnlein #1029, 7-3/4", ca.1940. $175-$250.

Santa, Kutzscher, #13187, 7",
ca.1920. $300-$500.

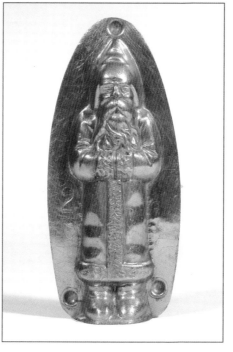

Santa hands in muff, 4",
ca.1940. $150-$200.

Santa, Anton Reiche #14786, 4",
ca.1920. $300-$500.

Santa, Jaburg #44, 7-1/2",
ca.1920. $250-$350.

Chalkware Santa by Wendy.
This was my first time painting.
Penny Burns taught me how
to paint in just a few hours!

Santa in chimney, Jaburg #55, 6",
ca.1920. $400-$650.

Additional view.

Four piece Santa with separate arm and bag, Anton Reiche #16703, 11", ca.1920. $2,000 and up.

Santa, Anton Reiche #27931, ca.1930. *Collection of Anne Launius.* $650 and up.

Santa in chimney, Weygandt, #433, 4-1/2", ca.1940. $300-$450.

Chalkware by Anne Launius.

Christmas

Boy with snowman, Anton Reiche #6866, 3-1/4", ca.1910. $450-$600.

Snowman, Anton Reiche #16582, 4-1/2", ca. 1925. $450-$600.

Snowman, Vormenfabriek #15276, 4-3/4", ca.1950. $150.

Chalkware by Moni's Folkart.

Snowman, Anton Reiche #32889, 5-1/4", ca.1930. $450.

Snowman, Létang, 10", ca.1940. $800.

Chalkware and photo courtesy of Moni's Folkart.

Snowman, Anton Reiche #28340, 4", ca.1920. $500-$650.

Small snowman. *Collection of Ginny Betourne.* $350-$450.

Chalkware by Ginny Betourne.

Snowman, Laurösch #4475, 5", ca.1930. $450-$550.

Gathering of snow people at Vaillancourt Folk Art Studios.

Snowman, Laurösch #3034, 6", ca. 1930. *Collection of Ginny Betourne.* $500-$600.

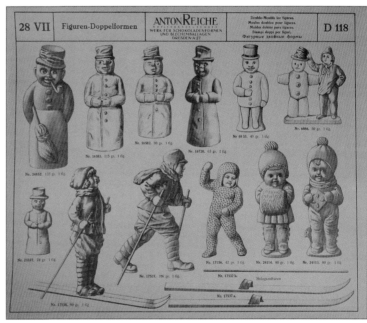

Page from original Anton Reiche catalog.

Snowman, 5-1/4", ca.1940. $400-$500.

Page from original Laurösch catalog.

Christmas tree with toys underneath, Hörnlein #1577, 6", ca.1950. $250.

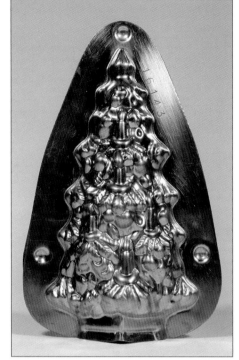

Christmas tree, Vormenfabriek #16143, 5 1/4", ca.1950. $150.

Small Christmas tree, Weygandt #562, 4", ca.1950. $150-$200.

Compliments of D. Ghirardelli Co. San Francisco, Cal.

Manufacturers of IMPERIAL COCOA AND OTHER HIGH GRADE COCOAS AND CHOCOLATES

Ghirardelli coloring book, ca.1920.

Angel, Hörnlein #1570, 5", ca.1940. $200-$300.

230

The tradition of hanging Christmas stockings is associated with a legend surrounding St. Nicholas. While St. Nicholas was in Asia Minor he heard of three sisters with no money for a dowry. One night he tossed a sack full of gold coins through the window of their house—enough for the oldest to marry. The second night he did the same for the middle daughter, but, on the third night when he arrived with his bag of gold the windows were locked. St. Nicholas climbed onto the roof and dropped the coins down the chimney. The coins landed in the stockings that were hung to dry by the fire. The story of this Christmas miracle spread throughout the world and stockings have been hung by chimneys at Christmas ever since.

Reverse side of stocking.

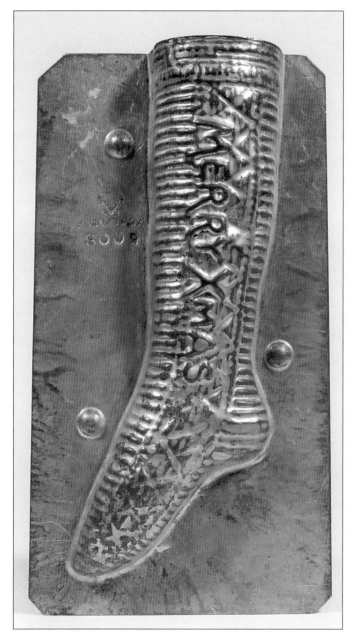

Stocking, Eppelsheimer #8009, 5-3/4", ca.1925. *Collection of Wendy Stys-Van Eimeren.* $250-$400.

Checking the stockings, Létang #4578, 4-1/2", ca.1930. $300-$450.

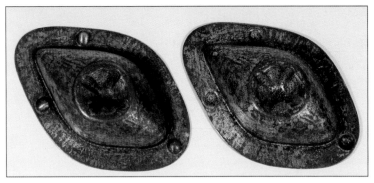

Christmas ornament, Anton Reiche #27544, 3-1/2",
ca.1920. *Collection of Carolyn Byrnes.* $250 and up.

Christmas ornament, Anton Reiche #26747, 2-1/2",
ca.1920. *Collection of Carolyn Byrnes.* $250 and up.

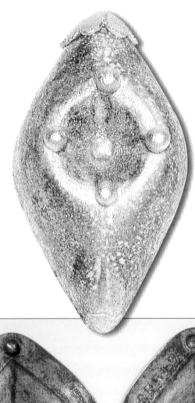

Chocolate by
Robert Twardzik of
RJT Extraordinary
Cakes & Confec-
tions NYC. Photo
by Marcus Pinto.

Chocolate by Robert
Twardzik. Photo by
Marcus Pinto.

Christmas ornament, Anton Reiche #27542, 3",
ca.1920. *Collection of Carolyn Byrnes.* $250 and up.

Christmas ornament, Anton Reiche
#27547, 3-1/2", ca.1920. *Collection
of Carolyn Byrnes.* $250 and up.

Chocolate by Robert
Twardzik. Photo by
Marcus Pinto.

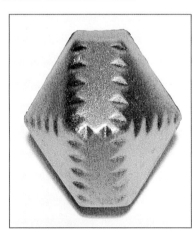

Chocolate by Robert
Twardzik. Photo by
Marcus Pinto.

Christmas ornament, Anton Reiche #27546, 3-1/2", ca.1920. *Collection of Carolyn Byrnes.* $250 and up.

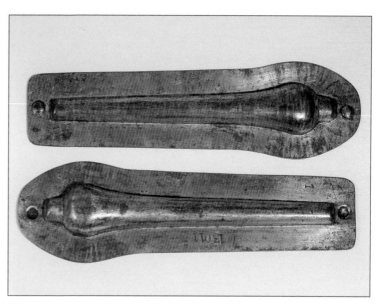

Christmas ornament, Anton Reiche #13011, 6-1/2", ca.1920. *Collection of Carolyn Byrnes.* $250 and up.

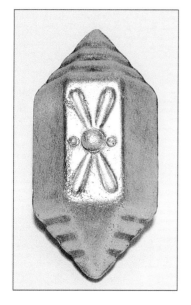

Chocolate by Robert Twardzik. Photo by Marcus Pinto.

Chocolate by Robert Twardzik. Photo by Marcus Pinto.

Christmas ornament, Anton Reiche #27545, 2-1/2", ca.1920. *Collection of Carolyn Byrnes.* $250 and up.

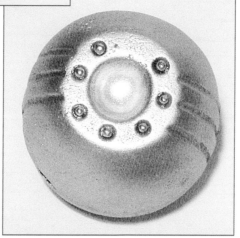

Chocolate by Robert Twardzik. Photo by Marcus Pinto.

Christmas ornament, Anton Reiche # 26746, 2-1/2", ca.1920. *Collection of Carolyn Byrnes.* $250 and up.

Chocolate by Robert Twardzik. Photo by Marcus Pinto.

233

Christmas ornament, Anton Reiche #27646, 3", ca.1920. *Collection of Carolyn Byrnes.* $250 and up.

In AD 350, Pope Julius I decreed that December 25 would be the official day to commemorate the birth of Jesus.

Crèche postcard style mold. *Collection and photo by Erwin and Monika Gschwind.*

Chocolate by Robert Twardzik. Photo by Marcus Pinto.

Crèche, Walters #5329, 6-1/4", ca.1920. *Collection of Paul & Fredricka Schwanka.* $500 and up.

Chocolate by Robert Twardzik. Photo by Marcus Pinto.

Reverse side of crèche.

Molded chocolate crèche and photo by Betsy Schoettlin of Serendipity Chocolates.

Mini crèche, Walter, 3-1/2", ca.1930. $350-$500.

Crèche, LeCerf #611, 11" x 16-3/4", ca.1930. *Collection of Carolyn Byrnes.* $3,000-$5,000.

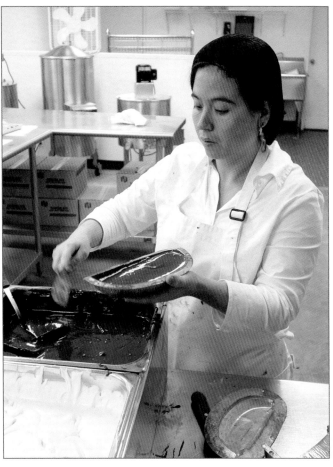

Rocio Estrada filling a crèche mold with tempered chocolate at Morgen Chocolate in Dallas.

Releasing the molded chocolate crèche.

Tapping out excess chocolate from the mold.

Four piece crèche, Létang, 6", ca.1930. *Collection of Rex Morgen.* $3,000 and up.

Objects

Frederic Bartholdi, the well known sculptor who designed the Statue of Liberty, also made the master mold for this banquet ice cream mold in 1875. This mold was used on July 4, 1876 during the Philadelphia Centennial Exposition at the fundraising banquet for the Statue of Liberty pedestal.

Close-up of Statue of Liberty face plate.

Statue of Liberty, 37" banquet ice cream mold. Only three are known to exist. *Courtesy of the Alice R. Stallings Memorial Foundation.*

Detail of face.

Molds on display at the Copia Museum in Napa, California, including the Statue of Liberty.

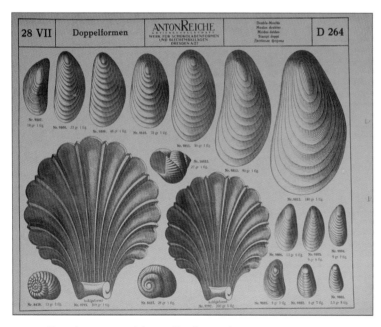

Page from original Anton Reiche catalog.

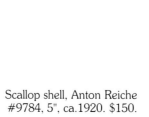

Scallop shell, Anton Reiche #9784, 5", ca.1920. $150.

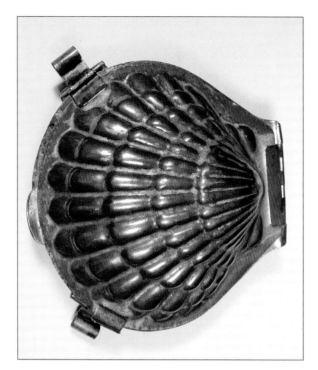

Scallop shell, 6", ca.1920. *Collection of Diane Cazalet.* $200-$300.

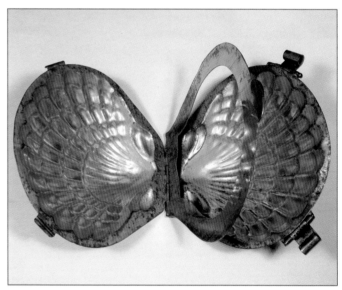

Inside view.

Barley sucker by Dorothy Timberlake Candies.

Large shell, Anton Reiche #9794, 9", ca.1920. $250.

Soap by Jamie Badore.

Additional view.

Oyster shell, inside view.

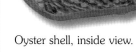

Oyster shell, Létang #1602, 3-1/2", ca.1900. $250.

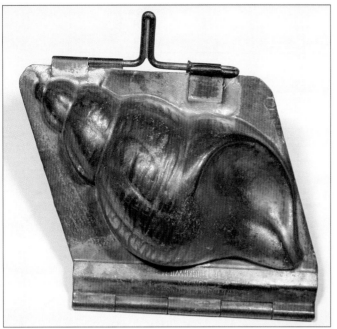

Conch shell, Teich, 3-1/2", ca.1920.
Collection of Diane Cazalet. $200-$300.

Large mussel shell, Anton Reiche, 6", ca.1930. $150-$200.

Snail shell, 2-1/2", ca.1920.
Collection of Diane Cazalet.
$150-$250.

Barley candy by Dorothy Timberlake Candies.

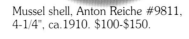

Mussel shell, Anton Reiche #9811,
4-1/4", ca.1910. $100-$150.

Three piece box, Anton Reiche #17655, 10", ca.1920. $350-$500.

Box with fruit design, Anton Reiche #17654, 6-1/2", ca.1920. *Collection of Carolyn Byrnes.* $200-$300.

Additional view.

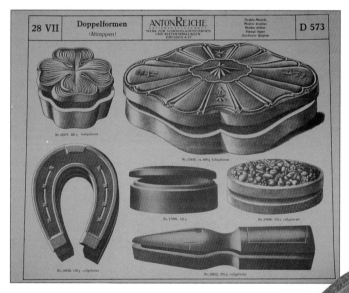

Page from original Anton Reiche catalog.

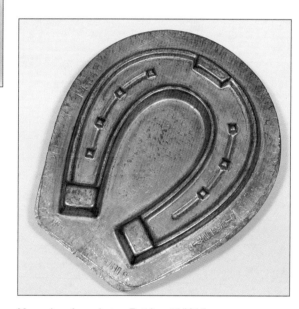

Horseshoe box, Anton Reiche #14915, 6", ca.1920. *Collection of Diane Cazalet.* $200-$250.

Three piece heart box, Anton Reiche #23245, 6", ca.1920. $200-$300.

Two piece heart boxes, German, ca.1920. Large box marked, "To my Valentine," 8"; small box marked, "To my Valentine," 6". $150 and $200.

Soap by Jamie Badore.

Heart box, 3", ca.1920. *Collection of Carolyn Byrnes.* $150.

Heart with coin, 7", ca.1930. *Collection of Diane Cazalet.* $150-$200.

Chocolate by Morgen Chocolate.

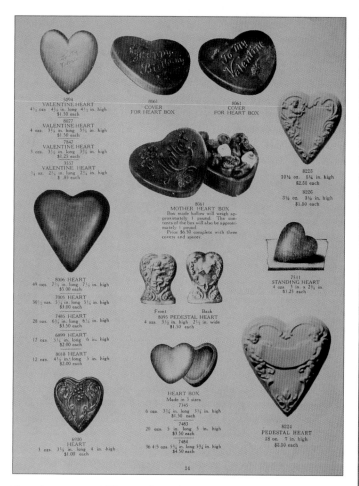

Page from original Weygandt catalog.

Heart on pedestal, Eppelsheimer #8095, 6", ca.1940.
Collection of Rex Morgen. $250-$350.

Reverse side.

Heart postcard style mold, 5-1/2", ca.1930.
Collection of Rex Morgen. $350-$500.

Chocolate by Morgen Chocolate.

Crown, Randle & Smith #167, 5-1/2", ca.1930.
Collection of Diane Cazalet. $250-$400.

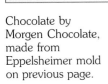

Flat mold of crowns, Létang #1530, 8" x 6", ca.1920. *Collection of Carolyn Byrnes.* $150-$200.

Chocolate by Morgen Chocolate, made from Eppelsheimer mold on previous page.

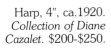

Harp, 4", ca.1920. *Collection of Diane Cazalet.* $200-$250.

Cast castle mold.

Soap by Jamie Badore.

Cast mold exterior, 5", ca.1940.
Collection of Carolyn Byrnes. $250.

Temple, Anton Reiche #26418, 4", ca.1920.
Collection of Diane Cazalet. $350 and up.

Reverse side.

French trade cards
for Chocolat
Guerin-Boutron.

Four piece shoe, #2609, 8", ca.1950. $300-$450.

Side view.

Sole.

Tongue.

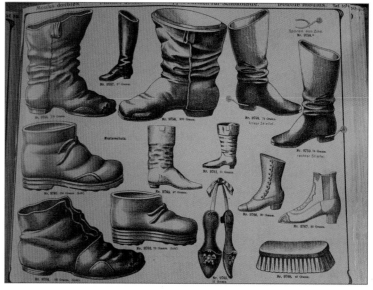

Page from original Anton Reiche catalog.
Collection of Monica Tinhofer.

Boot, Anton Reiche #9758, 4", ca.1920. *Collection of Diane Cazalet.* $150.

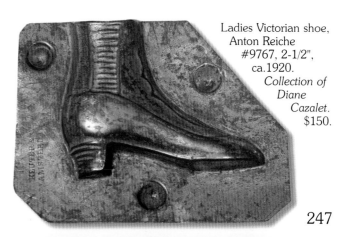

Ladies Victorian shoe, Anton Reiche #9767, 2-1/2", ca.1920. *Collection of Diane Cazalet.* $150.

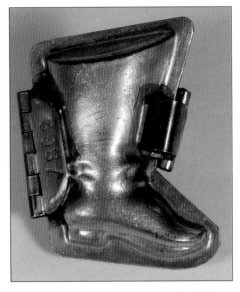

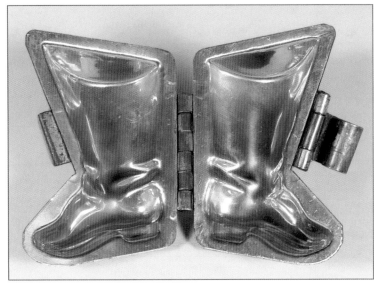

Small boot, #3987, 2-1/4", ca.1920. $125.   Inside view of small boot.

Victorian boot, Anton Reiche #9766, 3", ca.1920. *Collection and photo courtesy of William Timberlake M.D.* $150.

Boot, Amsterdam, 3", ca.1920. $125.

Chocolate advertisement.

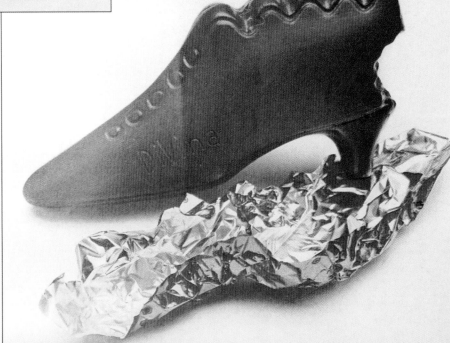

Art Deco shoe, Anton Reiche, ca.1930.
Collection of Rex Morgen. $150-$200.

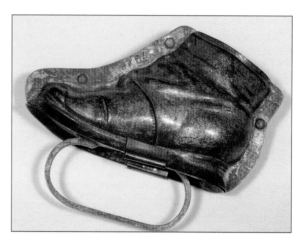

Three piece shoe, Anton Reiche #9762,
5-1/2", ca.1910. $150-$200.

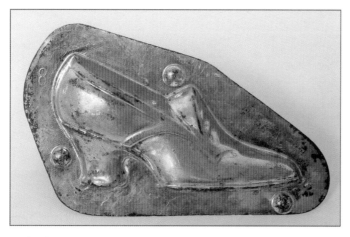

Ladies high heel shoe, ca.1930.
Collection of Rex Morgen. $150-$200.

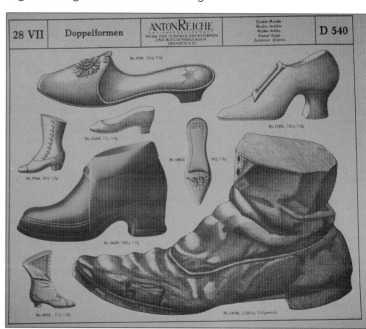

Baby shoe, #7926, 5-1/2", ca.1910.
Collection of Diane Cazalet. $150-$200.

Page from original Anton Reiche catalog.

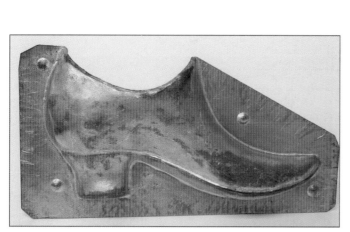

Shoe, Eppelsheimer #8033, 7", ca.1920.
Collection of Rex Morgen. $75-$100.

Children in different parts of Europe leave clogs for St. Nicholas on the windowsill or outside their bedroom doors at Christmas. In the morning, they hope to find that St. Nicholas has filled their shoes with oranges, apples, nuts, sweets, and small toys.

Floral life-sized clog, Anton Reiche #13041, 10", ca.1920. $150.

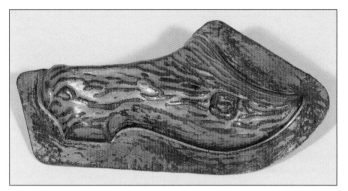

Wood grain clog, Létang #992, 4-1/2", ca.1920. $75.

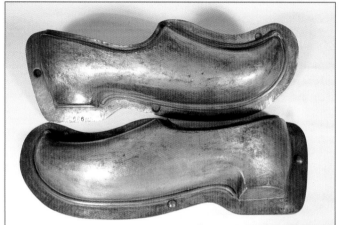

Large clog, Anton Reiche #14939, 12", ca.1920. $175.

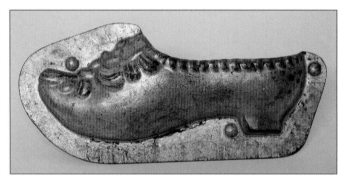

Floral accent clog, ca.1920. *Collection of Rex Morgen.* $150.

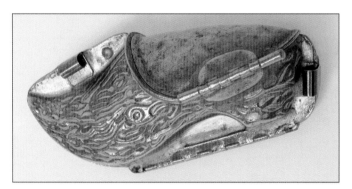

Hinged mini wood grain clog, 3", ca.1920. *Collection of Rex Morgen.* $75.

Box of molded chocolate cat tongues from Vienna.

Cat tongues mold, Anton Reiche #1214, 6", ca.1920. $75.

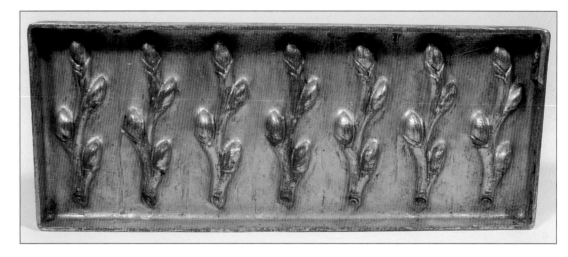

Flat of pussy willows, 7" x 3-1/2", ca.1910. *Collection of Carolyn Byrnes.* $150.

Chocolate Easter eggs advertisement from MacRobertson, Australia.

Egg, Eppelsheimer #4705, 3", ca.1920. $50.

Egg, Eppelsheimer #5027, 4 3/8", ca.1920. *Collection of Rex Morgen.* $50.

Egg, 5", ca.1920. *Collection of Carolyn Byrnes.* $75.

Soap by Jamie Badore.

251

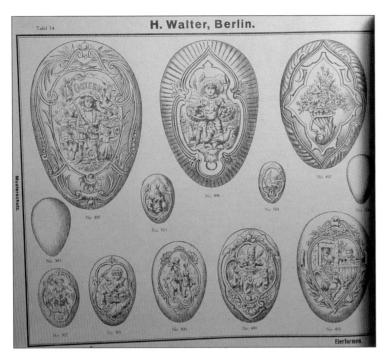

Page from original Hermann Walter catalog.

Soap by Jamie Badore.

Hinged egg, Anton Reiche #6240, 5-1/2", ca.1910. *Collection of Carolyn Byrnes.* $150.

Egg, Eppelsheimer #4699, 4-3/4", ca.1920. *Collection of Rex Morgen.* $50.

Additional view.

Egg, 3", ca.1920. *Collection of Rex Morgen.* $35.

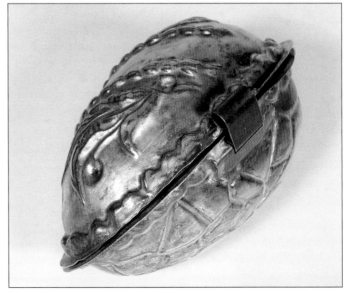

Assorted eggs; heart patterned egg marked
Anton Reiche #30979, 6", ca.1940. $75 each.

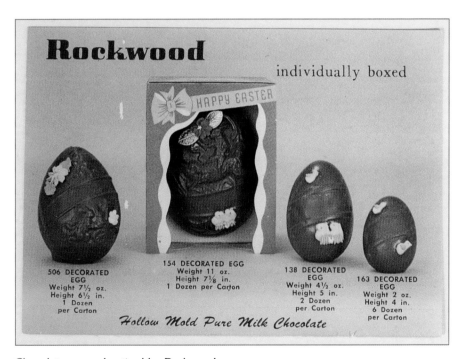

Chocolate eggs advertised by Rockwood.

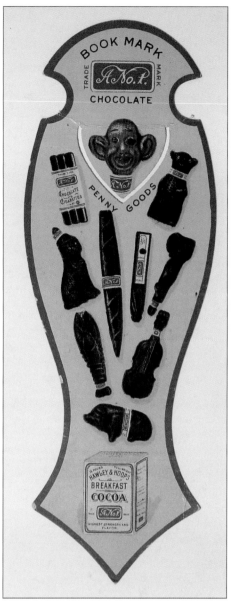

Molded chocolates bookmark
by Hawley & Hoops.

Cigar, Anton Reiche #14924,
8", ca.1920. *Collection of
Diane Cazalet*. $125.

253

Heavy mini cigar mold, Anton Reiche #787, 9-1/2", ca.1910. $125.

Hawley & Hoops trade card advertising chocolate cigarettes.

Page from original Anton Reiche catalog.

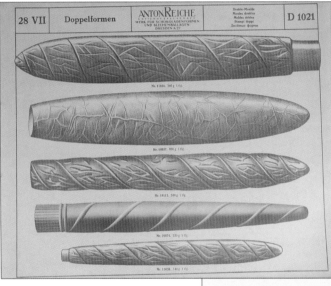

Ashtray, originally marked Eppelsheimer Molds for Chocolate.

Same ashtray, marked Thos. Mills Molds for Chocolate.

Boat with mast and paper sail, Létang #4769, 7", ca.1930.
Collection and translation by Carolyn Byrnes. $650 and up.

Ship, Anton Reiche #25946, 8", ca.1920.
Collection of Diane Cazalet. $300-$450.

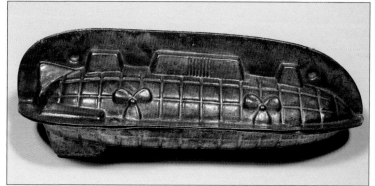

Submarine, Anton Reiche #10816, 8", ca.1920.
Collection of Diane Cazalet. $500 and up.

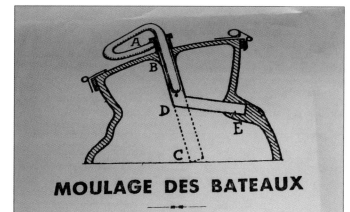

MOULAGE DES BATEAUX

Le dessus du moule étant fermé, introduire la goupille **A** dans son logement comme l'indique le dessin.

Enfiler ensuite le tube carton **B. C.** sur la partie dépassant à l'intérieur du moule. Mouler comme habituellement en ayant soin de garnir largement en **B.**

Plier l'extrémité du tube carton suivant **D. E.** et fixer en **E** avec du chocolat.

Directions for assembling boat from Létang:
With the top of the mold closed, put pin A into the hole according to the drawing. Then open the mold and put the cardboard tube B. C. on the pin. Mold the top with chocolate as usual, taking care to cover B. Then fold the end of the cardboard tube in position D.E. and affix with chocolate.

Hot rod in chocolate and photo courtesy of Calico Chocolates.

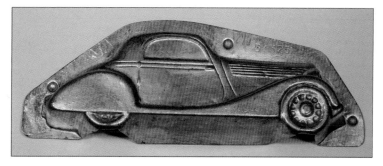

Car, Anton Reiche #34325, 5-1/2", ca.1940.
Collection of Diane Cazalet. $150.

Shell Oil tanker, Kutzscher #12561, 3", ca.1920. $75.

Vintage postcard.

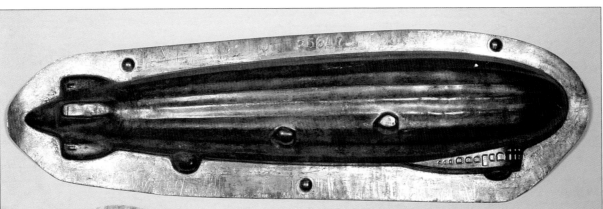

Zeppelin, Anton Reiche #25647, 11", ca.1920. *Collection of Diane Cazalet.* $500 and up.

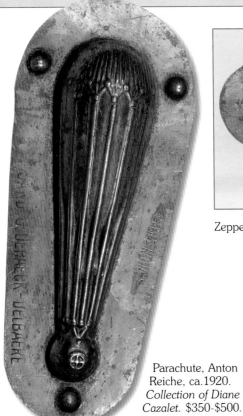

Parachute, Anton Reiche, ca.1920. *Collection of Diane Cazalet.* $350-$500.

Zeppelin, Kutzscher #5555, 7-1/2", ca.1920. $500 and up.

Zeppelin, Anton Reiche #7962, 7", ca.1910. *Collection of Diane Cazalet.* $500 and up.

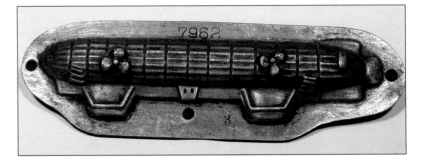

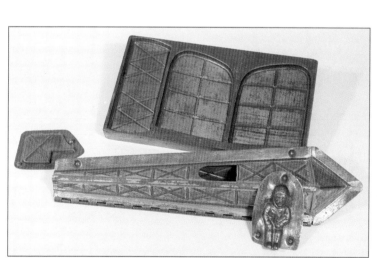

Hot air balloon, Kutzscher #5646, 3-1/2",
ca.1920. *Collection of Diane Cazalet.*
$200-$250.

Hermann Walter advertisement.

Chocolate and photo courtesy
of Serendipity Chocolates.

Multi-piece plane, Kutzscher #5599, pilot #5617, 11-1/2",
ca.1920. *Collection of Carolyn Byrnes.* $800 and up.

Page from original
Kutzscher catalog.

Pocket watch, Anton Reiche #9926, 4",
ca.1920. $200-$250.

Key, Anton Reiche #9856, 15", ca.1920.
Collection of Diane Cazalet. $800 and up.

Saber, Anton Reiche #10012, 10".
Collection of Diane Cazalet. $200-$300.

Padlock, Anton Reiche #9849,
5", ca.1920. *Collection of
Diane Cazalet.* $150-$250.

Binoculars, Kutzscher #5611,
3", ca.1920. $250.

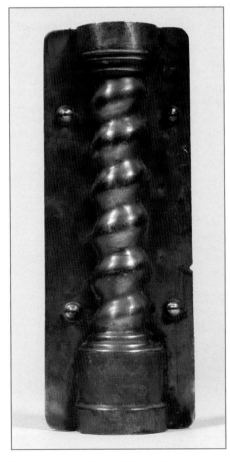

Pocket knife, Anton Reiche #30598, 5", ca.1930.
Collection of my son Jericho. $150.

Brass column, 6", ca.1930. *Collection
of Carolyn Byrnes.* $150.

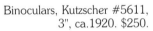

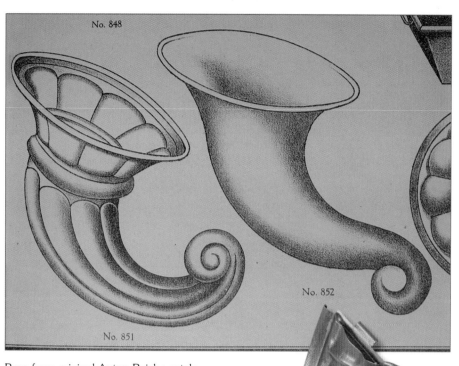

Page from original Anton Reiche catalog.

Box, Anton Reiche #10072, 5-1/2",
ca.1920. *Collection of Diane Cazalet.*
$150-$250.

Inside view.

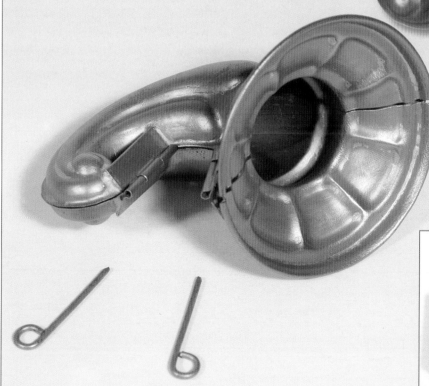

Cornucopia, 5", ca.1920. $250-$350.

Box, Létang #4256, 5", ca.1920. *Collection of Diane Cazalet.* $250-$350.

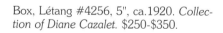

Chocolate by Morgen Chocolate.

Umbrella, Anton Reiche #26417, 7", ca.1920. *Collection of Carolyn Byrnes.* $150.

Alligator purse, Anton Reiche #23721, 4", ca.1920. $250-$350.

Cross, Eppelsheimer #8096, 5-1/2", ca.1940. *Collection of Rex Morgen.* $150-$200.

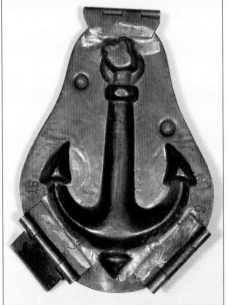

Anchor, Anton Reiche #6867, 5-1/2", ca.1920. *Collection of Diane Cazalet.* $150-$200.

Lighthouse, Anton Reiche #14057, 3-3/4", ca.1920. $150.

Lighthouse flat, Anton Reiche, 3-1/2" x 7-1/2", ca.1910.
Collection of Carolyn Byrnes. $150.

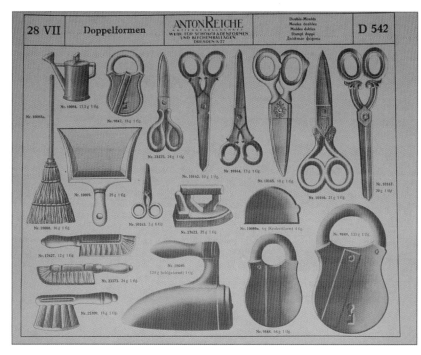

Page from original Anton Reiche catalog.

Mirror, #2576, 4",
ca.1920. *Collection
of Diane Cazalet.*
$150.

Iron, Anton Reiche #10083, 4", ca.1920.
Collection of Diane Cazalet. $100-$150.

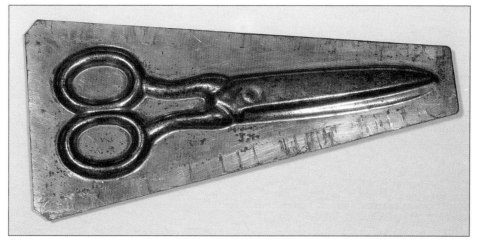

Scissors, Anton Reiche #23375, 5", ca.1920.
Collection of Diane Cazalet. $150-$200.

Dustpan, Anton Reiche #10089, ca.1920. *Collection of Diane Cazalet.* $100-$150.

Top, Anton Reiche #9730, 5", ca.1920. $100-$200.

Brush, Anton Reiche #16796, 8", ca.1920. *Collection of Diane Cazalet.* $150-$200.

Football, Anton Reiche #17548, 3", ca.1920. *Collection of Diane Cazalet.* $100-$150.

Stollwerck's trade cards.

Dominoes flat, Létang #194, 8" x 10", ca.1930.
Collection of Carolyn Byrnes. $150-$250.

Maillard's trade card.

"The Love Game," Létang #290, 4 5/8", ca.1920. *Collection of Carolyn Byrnes.* $200-$300. This would be made in chocolate with a cardboard accessory arrow spinner placed in the middle. It is based essentially on a love game. Here is the story: Marguerite is a flower (daisy). "Effeuiller" means you take the leaves off...here the petals off. You take them off while you sing "je t'aime...un peu (first petal), beaucoup (second petal), passionnément, à la folie, pas du tout." When the last petal is off, you stop on the word...if it is, for example "pas du tout," it means you don't love the person. The translation is: "I love you...a little bit, a lot, passionately, to become mad, not at all." Story and translation by Laure Dorchy.

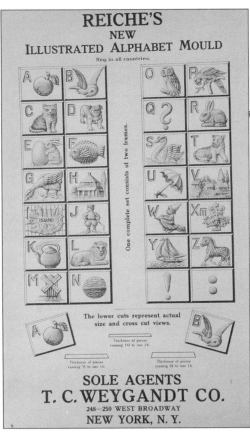

Anton Reiche advertisement.

Chocolat Guerin-Boutron trade cards.

Alphabet flat, Anton Reiche #30700-30725, 10" x 12", ca.1930. $250-$350.

264

Overstuffed chair, Anton Reiche #25907, 5", ca.1920. *Collection of Diane Cazalet.* $400 and up.

Scale, Anton Reiche #28409, 3-1/4", ca.1930. *Collection of Diane Cazalet.* $150.

Light bulb, Anton Reiche #10820, 4", ca.1920. *Collection of Diane Cazalet.* $100.

Bassinet, Walter #9938, 4", ca.1930. *Collection of Carolyn Byrnes.* $150-$250.

Coffee pot, Anton Reiche #1075, 3-1/2", ca.1920. *Collection of Diane Cazalet.* $150.

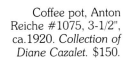

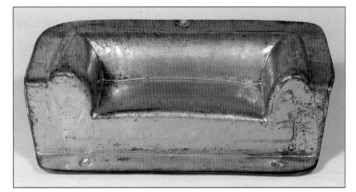

Sofa, Anton Reiche #24952, 8", ca.1920. *Collection of Carolyn Byrnes.* $450 and up.

Soap by Jamie Badore.

Peas in pod, Anton Reiche #9666, 3-1/2",
ca.1920. *Collection of Diane Cazalet.* $125.

Pine cone, Anton Reiche #7948, 7-1/2", ca.1910.
Collection of Carolyn Byrnes. $150.

Pineapple, Sommet, 3-1/2", ca.1920.
Collection of Diane Cazalet. $125.

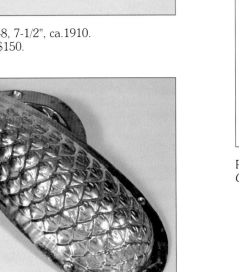

Additional view.

Peach slice, Sommet
#1764, 2-1/2", ca.1930.
*Collection of Diane
Cazalet.* $125.

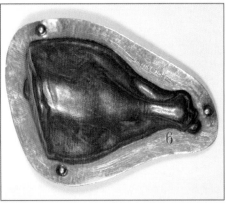

Ham hock, Anton Reiche #9427, 4",
ca.1920. *Collection of Diane Cazalet.* $150.

Statue of Liberty flat, 8", ca.1920. *Collection of Monica Tinhofer.* $250 and up.

Ghirardelli flat, 8", ca.1930. $150.

Flat with assorted medallions, Anton Reiche, 10" x 13", ca.1920. *Collection of Carolyn Byrnes.* $175.

Eiffel Tower, Marie Létang, 27". Collection and photo courtesy of William Timberlake M.D. $5,000 and up.

Chocolat Guerin-Boutron trade card.

Page from original Létang catalog.

Collector's Tips and Closing

Antique chocolate mold collecting can be an exciting and incomparable diversion! There are however, a few things to consider when making additions to your collection.

When purchasing an antique chocolate mold, look for front and back pieces that line up properly. Check the lot numbers stamped on the front and back of the mold; these should be the same—for example, #45 marked on the front half of the mold and #45 marked on the back half. Occasionally you will find molds that have been part of a large collection with many duplicates. If the previous owners were not careful to match the molds with correct sets of fronts and backs you may end up with a mold that does not line up and may not produce the correct three-dimensional form.

Mismatched chocolate molds or molds with damage, holes, rust, and poor re-tinning jobs can reduce the value of a mold as well as its functionality.

Molds can be gently cleaned using a Dremmel® type rotary tool with stainless steel cup shape brushes—please don't forget to wear safety glasses. I also recommend Scotch-Brite® pads in the maroon color; they are wonderful for removing oxidation and light scratches.

The other side of the mold, not yet cleaned with the Scotch Brite® pad.

Steel bristled brushes are also good cleaners—be very careful not to scratch the mold with deep strokes. Test a small area first.

Remember, if you wash your mold you should make sure it dries thoroughly before putting it away or rust may form. If you use your oven to dry the mold make sure it is only for a few minutes at a very low temperature—solder used on some molds melts easily in the oven at warmer temperatures. Never go above 250° F.

If the mold will not be used for molding chocolate, WD-40® or similar oil based lubricants can be applied to protect the metal and prevent rust. Olive oil or mineral oil can also be used if you plan on using the molds for candy molding.

One side of this mold was quickly cleaned with a Scotch Brite® pad.

Létang, Matfer, and the American Chocolate Mould Co. are manufacturing new metal chocolate molds on original master dies and equipment. These new metal molds are inexpensive and can be safely used for chocolate or crafts, making them an ideal option for many enthusiasts.

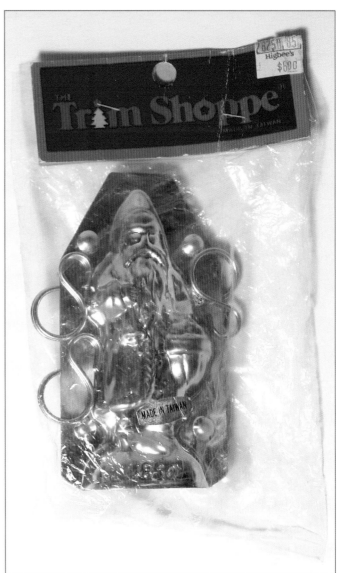

New sucker mold from antique design.

Metal chocolate molds are also being manufactured offshore, apparently for use as Christmas decorations, as seen in the photo at top right. Also in the United States, new metal chocolate molds are being manufactured and then "aged" or rusted to look old, also for decorating purposes. This can be a problem for collectors, as many of these "aged" molds are then sold as originals when they are not.

In the late 1960s, Adrienne Trouw and her husband Bas learned of a chocolate company that had gone out of business in the Netherlands. They ventured into the abandoned factory and found over 3,000 metal chocolate molds—some with chocolate still in them!

Adrienne wanted to introduce the American people to some of these charming metal chocolate mold designs, so she had approximately thirty different designs manufactured by Vormenfabriek of Holland. Vormenfabriek manufactured the "new" molds using the original tooling, and then stamped them with the original Vormenfabriek design numbers.

The manufacturing of this Mickey Mouse mold design sold by Holland Handicrafts
was discontinued due to objections from the Walt Disney Company.

The finished metal chocolate molds were then stamped with the new name, "Holland Handicrafts." The company is no longer in business today, however thousands of these collectible molds were imported into the United States during the 1970s to 1980s.

The value of antique chocolate molds will continue to rise as they become more difficult to find. Many of the large collections in Europe have already been sold as old-fashioned chocolatiers have retired. Antique chocolate molds are a great investment as antiques and of course as works of art.

When buying antique chocolate molds from antique shops expect the prices to be higher than those on eBay. Prices at flea markets, estate sales, and auctions will gen-erally be the lowest. Prices will change due to economic conditions and will vary greatly depending on the condition of the mold.

The molds in this book have been measured from end to end including the flange.

In closing, I would like to say that working on this book has been an amazing experience and truly inspiring! Exciting adventures and so many unforgettable moments traveling throughout Europe and the United States will always remain prized and cherished memories. I have had the delightful opportunity to meet many beloved chocolate mold enthusiasts and am continuing to learn more about the ever-elusive antique chocolate molds! I hope you enjoyed the book and that life takes you on many treasured journeys.

Bibliography

Books

Divone, Judene. *Chocolate Moulds: A History & Encyclopedia*. Oakton, Virginia: Oakton Hills Publications, 1987.

Dorchy, Henry and Laure. *The Chocolate Mould*. Belgium: Éditions Ephéméra, 1999.

Mullen, Wendy. *Collector's Guide to Antique Chocolate Molds with Values*. USA: Hobby House Press, 2002.

Tinhofer, Monica, and Manfred Bachmann. *Osterhase, Nikolaus & Zeppelin*. Husum 1998.

Company Catalogs

Allmetal Catalog
Anton Reiche Catalog
Eppelsheimer Catalog
Heris Catalog

Hermann Walter Catalog
Jaburg Catalog
J.W. Allen Catalog
Kutzscher Catalog
Laurösch Catalog
Létang Catalog
Obermann Catalog
Reiner Fischer Catalog
Riecke Catalog
Savage Bros. Catalog
Thos.Mills Catalog
Weygandt Catalog
Willi Thormeier Magdeburg Catalog

Websites

St.NicholasCenter.org

Boy bunny in shorts and suspenders, Anton Reiche #29485, 12", ca. 1920. $450.

Vintage postcard.

Nr. 7833.
40 Gramm

Nr. 78
65 Gra

Nr. 7837. 500 Gramm.

Nr. 7838. 250 Gramm.

Nr. 7839. 165 Gramm.

N
5